Python for Problem Solvers

Crack Coding Interviews, Build Smart Solutions, and Think Like a Pro Coder

Booker Blunt

Rafael Sanders

Miguel Farmer

Boozman Richard

How to Scan a Barcode to Get a Repository

1. **Install a QR/Barcode Scanner** – Ensure you have a barcode or QR code scanner app installed on your smartphone or use a built-in scanner in **GitHub, GitLab, or Bitbucket.**

2. **Open the Scanner** – Launch the scanner app and grant necessary camera permissions.

3. **Scan the Barcode** – Align the barcode within the scanning frame. The scanner will automatically detect and process it.

4. **Follow the Link** – The scanned result will display a **URL to the repository**. Tap the link to open it in your web browser or Git client.

5. **Clone the Repository** – Use **Git clone** with the provided URL to download the repository to your local machine.

Chapter 1: Introduction to Python for Problem Solving

Overview of Python as a Problem-Solving Language

In today's world of rapid technological advancement, problem-solving has become the core of software development. Every coding challenge, from creating apps to automating tasks, hinges on the ability to break problems down and develop efficient solutions. When it comes to choosing a language that seamlessly blends simplicity, versatility, and power, Python consistently stands out as the go-to choice for coders and problem solvers alike.

Why is Python the language of choice for so many? It's simple: Python is accessible. This programming language was designed with the idea of readability and ease of use at its core. It's one of the most beginner-friendly languages available, yet it's also powerful enough to handle some of the most complex systems in the world. Whether you're just starting your coding journey or you're an experienced developer working on large-scale applications, Python provides a flexible platform to approach and solve a vast array of problems.

Python's appeal is multifaceted. First, it has a clean, readable syntax that makes it easier to learn and apply. Unlike languages that require complex syntactical structures or cumbersome semicolons, Python's straightforward approach to writing code allows developers to focus on logic and problem-solving rather than struggling with the language itself. This focus on readability not only makes Python accessible for beginners, but it also makes it highly maintainable. Developers can work collaboratively on projects, and the code remains easy to understand for others, even after long periods of time.

Another key advantage of Python is its extensive ecosystem. With thousands of libraries and frameworks available, Python can be used to tackle a wide range of problems. From web development to machine learning, from data analysis to network programming, Python has a solution waiting in the wings. The language has been designed to be general-purpose, meaning it doesn't lock you into any specific area of programming. This flexibility is a big reason why Python has been adopted by everyone from hobbyists to major tech companies like Google, Facebook, and NASA.

In this chapter, we will explore how Python's simplicity and power make it the ideal language for problem solvers. We'll dive into the language's basic syntax, learn how to set up your Python environment, and write your very first program. By the end of this chapter, you will not only understand why Python is so popular but will also be ready to jump into the world of problem-solving with Python.

Why Python is the Go-To Language for Problem Solvers and Coders

To truly grasp Python's value as a problem-solving language, we need to understand what makes it stand out from the pack. Python isn't just another programming language; it's a tool designed with problem solvers in mind. Let's break down some of the factors that make Python ideal for tackling real-world challenges.

Simplicity and Readability

First and foremost, Python's syntax is incredibly simple. While many programming languages tend to use complex structures and excessive punctuation, Python uses straightforward and readable code. You won't find yourself spending hours searching for missing semicolons or brackets, nor will you have to learn dozens of advanced syntax rules just to write a simple program. This simplicity is what makes Python so appealing to beginners, but it's also what makes it such a powerful tool for professionals.

The language prioritizes readability, which means it's easy for anyone to pick up and understand code. When writing Python, the intention is clear: you write what you want to express in as few characters as possible, without the need for excessive boilerplate code. This feature allows developers to focus on the logic of the problem they're trying to solve, rather than being bogged down by complicated language rules.

A Large Standard Library and Third-Party Modules

Python's power doesn't just come from its simplicity—it also comes from its extensive ecosystem of libraries and modules. These are pre-written pieces of code that you can use to perform tasks without having to reinvent the wheel. For example, if you want to perform complex mathematical calculations, you don't need to write the algorithms yourself; you can simply use Python's built-in `math` module.

Beyond the standard library, Python boasts a vibrant ecosystem of third-party libraries that allow developers to extend the language's capabilities even further. Libraries like NumPy for numerical computing, Pandas for data analysis, and Flask for web development make Python a versatile tool for solving almost any problem. Python's package index, PyPI, contains thousands of open-source libraries for just about every field you can imagine. Whether you're working with data, web scraping, or building machine learning models, chances are Python has a tool for the job.

Cross-Platform Compatibility

Another important factor in Python's popularity is its cross-platform compatibility. Whether you're working on a Windows PC, a Mac, or a Linux machine, you can run Python code seamlessly across all these platforms. This makes Python an ideal choice for developers who want to write code that can be executed in different environments without major modifications. The ability to write code once and run it anywhere is crucial for solving problems in today's interconnected, multi-platform world.

Community Support and Resources

The Python community is vast and incredibly supportive. From online forums to Stack Overflow, from tutorials to blogs, there are countless resources available to help developers troubleshoot problems, learn new concepts, and advance their skills. The Python community is known for being friendly and inclusive, which is a huge plus for newcomers to the language. Whether you're stuck on a problem or looking for a way to optimize your code, there are communities and resources where you can get help.

Understanding Python Syntax and Basic Structures

Now that we've established why Python is such a powerful language for problem solvers, it's time to roll up our sleeves and dive into the syntax and basic structures that make Python so approachable.

Python's syntax is designed to be simple and intuitive. Let's start with the basics.

Variables and Data Types

In Python, variables are used to store values. These variables don't require explicit declarations like in other programming languages, meaning you don't need to specify the type of data they will hold. Python automatically infers the type based on the value assigned to the variable.

python

```
x = 5         # integer
y = 3.14      # floating-point number
name = "Python"  # string
is_active = True  # boolean
```

You can use these variables to perform operations or store results. For example, you can add two numbers, concatenate strings, or evaluate boolean expressions.

Basic Operations

Python supports a wide range of basic operations, including arithmetic, comparison, and logical operations.

- Arithmetic: +, -, *, /, // (floor division), % (modulus), ** (exponentiation)
- Comparison: ==, !=, >, <, >=, <=
- Logical: and, or, not

python

```
sum_result = 5 + 10      # 15
division_result = 10 / 3  # 3.333333...
is_greater = 5 > 3       # True
```

Python also allows you to combine operations in expressions to perform more complex calculations.

Control Flow: If-Else Statements

Python uses simple `if-else` statements to handle decision-making. This structure allows you to execute certain blocks of code based on whether a condition is true or false.

python

```
age = 20
if age >= 18:
    print("You are an adult.")
else:
    print("You are a minor.")
```

The `if` statement checks the condition, and if it's true, it runs the code within the block. Otherwise, the `else` block is executed.

Loops: Iterating Over Data

Python supports two types of loops: `for` and `while`. The `for` loop is used to iterate over a sequence (like a list, tuple, or string), while the `while` loop continues executing as long as a condition is true.

python

```
# Using a for loop to iterate over a list
for i in [1, 2, 3, 4, 5]:
    print(i)

# Using a while loop to print numbers less than 5
num = 0
while num < 5:
    print(num)
```

```
num += 1
```

Functions: Reusable Blocks of Code

Functions in Python are defined using the `def` keyword and are used to group together a set of instructions that perform a specific task. Functions help make code more modular and reusable.

```python
python

def greet(name):
    return f"Hello, {name}!"

print(greet("Alice"))   # Output: Hello, Alice!
```

Setting Up Your Python Environment and Tools

Before you start writing Python code, you need to set up your development environment. This includes installing Python, choosing an editor or IDE, and setting up any additional tools or libraries you may need.

Installing Python

The first step is installing Python on your machine. Python can be downloaded from the official website (https://www.python.org/downloads/). The installation process is straightforward: just download the installer for your operating system, run it, and follow the on-screen instructions.

Once Python is installed, you can check the installation by opening a terminal or command prompt and typing:

```css
css

python --version
```

This should display the installed version of Python, confirming that everything is set up correctly.

Choosing an Editor or IDE

Python can be written in any text editor, but for a better experience, it's recommended to use an Integrated Development Environment (IDE) or a code editor that supports Python syntax highlighting, debugging, and other features. Some popular Python IDEs and editors include:

- **PyCharm**: A powerful, feature-rich IDE for Python development.
- **VS Code**: A lightweight, extensible editor with great Python support through extensions.
- **Jupyter Notebook**: Ideal for data science and machine learning projects, offering an interactive development environment.

Running Your First Python Program

Once you have Python set up and an editor ready, you can write your first Python program. Open your chosen editor and create a new file with the `.py` extension (e.g., `hello_world.py`). In the file, type the following code:

```python
print("Hello, World!")
```

Save the file and run it. If you're using an IDE, there will be a "Run" button to execute your program. If you're using the terminal, you can run the program by typing:

```nginx
```

```
python hello_world.py
```

When executed, Python will print the message "Hello, World!" to the console, marking the successful completion of your first program.

Hands-On Example: Install Python and Write Your First "Hello World" Program

As we've discussed, getting started with Python is as simple as installing the language, setting up an editor, and writing a few lines of code. By now, you should have Python installed and your editor ready to go. You've also seen how to create a simple "Hello World" program.

Take a moment to write and run your first Python program. Don't worry if you encounter any issues—this is all part of the learning process. With Python, solving problems becomes an enjoyable and rewarding experience.

Chapter 2: Mastering Python Data Structures

Understanding Basic Data Structures: Lists, Tuples, Sets, and Dictionaries

Data structures form the backbone of any software solution. They are essential for storing, organizing, and processing data efficiently. As a Python programmer, understanding how and when to use various data structures is key to solving problems efficiently and effectively. In this chapter, we will explore Python's most fundamental data structures: **lists, tuples, sets**, and **dictionaries**. By the end of this chapter, you will have a deep understanding of how these structures work and how to leverage them to solve real-world problems.

What are Data Structures?

In simple terms, data structures are ways of organizing and storing data in a computer so that it can be accessed and modified efficiently. The choice of data structure has a direct impact on the performance of a program, influencing how fast and efficiently a program runs. While some data structures are designed for general use, others are more specialized to handle specific types of data.

Data structures are not just abstract concepts—they are practical tools that help developers write optimized and maintainable code. They allow you to manage data in a way that makes it easy to perform operations like insertion, deletion, searching, and sorting.

Lists: Ordered, Mutable Collections

One of the most commonly used data structures in Python is the **list**. A list is an ordered collection of items, which means the order of elements is preserved. Lists are **mutable**, which means you can modify their contents after they are created. Lists can contain items of different types—integers, strings, objects—allowing for great flexibility in the types of data they hold.

Key Features of Lists:

- **Ordered**: The elements in a list have a defined order, and this order is preserved. This allows for indexing and slicing.
- **Mutable**: Lists can be changed by adding, removing, or modifying elements.
- **Flexible**: Lists can hold items of any data type, and these items don't need to be of the same type.

Syntax for Lists:

Creating a list is simple in Python. Lists are enclosed in square brackets, and items are separated by commas.

```python
my_list = [1, 2, 3, 4, 5]   # A list of integers
mixed_list = [1, "Python", 3.14, True]   # A list with different data types
```

You can access the elements of a list using indices, starting from 0.

```python
print(my_list[0])   # Output: 1
```

Python also supports negative indexing, where -1 refers to the last item in the list, -2 to the second-to-last, and so on.

```python
```

```python
print(my_list[-1])   # Output: 5
```

Common Operations on Lists:

1. **Appending Elements**: You can add elements to the end of a list using the `append()` method.

```python
```

```python
my_list.append(6)   # Adds 6 to the end of the list
```

2. **Inserting Elements**: The `insert()` method allows you to insert an element at a specific index.

```python
```

```python
my_list.insert(2, 7)   # Inserts 7 at index 2
```

3. **Removing Elements**: The `remove()` method removes the first occurrence of a specified item.

```python
```

```python
my_list.remove(3)   # Removes the first occurrence of 3
```

4. **Slicing**: Lists can be sliced to get a sublist.

```python
```

```python
sublist = my_list[1:4]   # Gets a sublist from index 1 to 3
```

5. **Sorting**: The `sort()` method sorts the elements in place.

```python
my_list.sort()  # Sorts the list in ascending order
```

Use Cases for Lists: Lists are best suited for scenarios where:

- You need to maintain an ordered collection of items.
- The items in the collection can change over time (i.e., you need to add, remove, or modify items).
- You need to store heterogeneous data (different types of elements).

Tuples: Immutable, Ordered Collections

A **tuple** is very similar to a list, but with one major difference: tuples are **immutable**, meaning that once a tuple is created, its elements cannot be modified. This property makes tuples useful in situations where you want to ensure that the data remains unchanged.

Key Features of Tuples:

- **Ordered**: Like lists, tuples maintain the order of their elements.
- **Immutable**: Once created, the elements of a tuple cannot be altered.
- **Fixed Size**: Since tuples are immutable, they have a fixed size, unlike lists.

Syntax for Tuples:

Tuples are defined using parentheses instead of square brackets.

```python
```

```python
my_tuple = (1, 2, 3, 4, 5)   # A tuple of integers
```

You can access tuple elements using indices, just like lists.

python

```python
print(my_tuple[0])   # Output: 1
```

However, you cannot modify a tuple after it is created.

python

```python
my_tuple[1] = 6   # This will raise a TypeError
```

Common Operations on Tuples:

1. **Concatenation**: You can concatenate two tuples using the + operator.

python

```python
new_tuple = my_tuple + (6, 7)   # Concatenates (6, 7)
to the tuple
```

2. **Repetition**: You can repeat a tuple using the * operator.

python

```python
repeated_tuple = my_tuple * 2   # Repeats the tuple
twice
```

3. **Slicing**: Like lists, tuples support slicing.

python

```python
sub_tuple = my_tuple[1:4]   # Gets a subtuple from
index 1 to 3
```

Use Cases for Tuples: Tuples are often used when:

- You need an ordered collection of items that should not change (e.g., coordinates in a 2D plane).
- You want to store data in a fixed, immutable structure for safety.
- You need to use the data as a key in dictionaries (since tuples are hashable, unlike lists).

Sets: Unordered Collections with Unique Elements

A **set** is an unordered collection of unique elements. Unlike lists and tuples, sets do not maintain the order of their elements, and they do not allow duplicate items. This makes sets ideal for scenarios where you need to store a collection of items without worrying about order or duplicates.

Key Features of Sets:

- **Unordered**: Sets do not maintain the order of their elements.
- **Unique**: A set can only contain unique items; duplicates are automatically removed.
- **Mutable**: You can add or remove items from a set.

Syntax for Sets:

You can create a set using curly braces `{}` or the `set()` constructor.

```python
my_set = {1, 2, 3, 4, 5}  # A set of integers
empty_set = set()  # An empty set
```

Common Operations on Sets:

1. **Adding Elements**: You can add elements to a set using the `add()` method.

```python
my_set.add(6)   # Adds 6 to the set
```

2. **Removing Elements**: The `remove()` method removes an element, but raises a KeyError if the element is not found.

```python
my_set.remove(3)   # Removes 3 from the set
```

3. **Set Operations**: Sets support mathematical set operations like union, intersection, and difference.

```python
another_set = {4, 5, 6, 7}
union_set = my_set | another_set   # Union of two sets
intersection_set = my_set & another_set   #
Intersection of two sets
difference_set = my_set - another_set   # Difference
between two sets
```

Use Cases for Sets: Sets are ideal when:

- You need to store a collection of unique items.
- You need to perform set operations like unions or intersections.
- You don't need to preserve the order of elements.

Dictionaries: Key-Value Pairs for Fast Lookups

A **dictionary** is a collection of key-value pairs. Unlike lists and tuples, which use numeric indices, dictionaries use **keys** to store and retrieve values. Each key in a dictionary must be unique, and the associated value can be any data type. Dictionaries are one of the most powerful data structures in Python because they provide **fast lookups** and can be used to store data efficiently.

Key Features of Dictionaries:

- **Key-Value Pairs**: A dictionary stores data as key-value pairs, where each key is unique.
- **Unordered**: Like sets, dictionaries do not guarantee the order of elements (though this has changed in Python 3.7+, where dictionaries maintain insertion order).
- **Mutable**: You can modify a dictionary by adding, removing, or updating key-value pairs.

Syntax for Dictionaries:

Dictionaries are defined using curly braces `{}` and the key-value pairs are separated by a colon `:`.

python

```python
my_dict = {"name": "Alice", "age": 25, "location": "New York"}
```

You can access dictionary values using their keys.

python

```python
print(my_dict["name"])  # Output: Alice
```

Common Operations on Dictionaries:

1. **Adding or Updating Key-Value Pairs**: You can add new key-value pairs or update existing ones.

```python
my_dict["email"] = "alice@example.com"  # Adds or
updates the key 'email'
```

2. **Removing Key-Value Pairs**: The `del` keyword can be used to remove a key-value pair.

```python
del my_dict["age"]  # Removes the key 'age'
```

3. **Iterating Over Dictionaries**: You can iterate over the keys, values, or key-value pairs in a dictionary.

```python
for key, value in my_dict.items():
    print(f"{key}: {value}")
```

Use Cases for Dictionaries: Dictionaries are best suited when:

- You need to store data in a **key-value** format.
- You need **fast lookups** based on unique keys.
- You need to associate related data, such as a name and age or product ID and price.

How to Choose the Right Data Structure for the Problem

Choosing the right data structure is crucial to solving a problem efficiently. The choice depends on several factors, including:

- **The type of data you're working with** (e.g., numbers, strings, objects).
- **The operations you need to perform** (e.g., adding elements, searching, deleting).
- **The size of the data** (e.g., are you working with a small or large dataset?).

As a general rule:

- Use **lists** when you need an ordered collection that can change over time.
- Use **tuples** when you need an ordered collection that should remain constant.
- Use **sets** when you need an unordered collection with unique elements.
- Use **dictionaries** when you need to map unique keys to corresponding values.

Time and Space Complexity of Common Data Structures

In this section, we'll take a closer look at the performance characteristics of these data structures in terms of **time complexity** (how long operations take) and **space complexity** (how much memory they use). Understanding these concepts is essential for optimizing your code and ensuring that it scales effectively.

Lists:

- **Time Complexity:**
    - **Access:** O(1) for accessing an element by index
    - **Search:** O(n) for finding an element
    - **Insertion/Deletion:** O(n) for adding or removing an item (since elements may need to be shifted)

Tuples:

- **Time Complexity:**
    - **Access:** O(1)
    - **Search:** O(n)
    - **Insertion/Deletion:** O(1) (tuples cannot be modified, so no insertion or deletion)

Sets:

- **Time Complexity:**
    - **Access/Search:** O(1)
    - **Insertion/Deletion:** O(1) (amortized time)

Dictionaries:

- **Time Complexity:**
    - **Access/Search:** O(1) for key-based access
    - **Insertion/Deletion:** O(1) for key-value pairs

In general, when working with lists, tuples, sets, and dictionaries, knowing how these data structures behave under the hood will guide you in selecting the most efficient one for your task.

Hands-On Example: Implementing a Python Program to Track Customer Orders

Let's put this knowledge into practice with a real-world example. We'll write a Python program that uses lists and dictionaries to track customer orders. The program will allow you to store information about customers and their orders and perform basic operations like adding new orders, updating orders, and viewing all customer orders.

Here's how you can start:

```python
# Initialize an empty dictionary to store customer
orders
customer_orders = {}

# Function to add a customer order
def add_order(customer_name, order_details):
    customer_orders[customer_name] = order_details

# Function to view orders
def view_orders():
    for customer, order in customer_orders.items():
        print(f"Customer: {customer}, Order:
{order}")

# Adding some customer orders
add_order("Alice", ["Laptop", "Mouse"])
add_order("Bob", ["Smartphone", "Headphones"])

# Viewing all orders
view_orders()
```

This basic program sets up a dictionary to store customer names as keys and order details as values (in the form of a list). You can easily expand this program to include more functionality, such as removing orders, updating them, or even storing additional information like prices.

Chapter 3: Control Flow and Loops for Efficient Problem Solving

Mastering if-else Statements, Loops, and List Comprehensions

As we venture deeper into the world of Python programming, the ability to control the flow of your code becomes critical. Control flow structures, such as conditional statements (if-else) and loops, allow you to dictate the path your program will follow based on the conditions you specify. These structures not only help make your code more dynamic but also enable it to solve a broader range of problems.

In this chapter, we will explore how to leverage Python's control flow mechanisms to write efficient and adaptable code. We will look at **if-else statements, loops,** and **list comprehensions,** which are essential tools in any programmer's toolkit. These structures will allow you to break down complex problems into manageable pieces, and by the end of this chapter, you'll understand how to use these tools in real-world applications to solve coding challenges effectively.

Understanding Control Flow in Python

Control flow refers to the order in which the individual instructions in a program are executed. In any program, the control flow determines which statements are executed based on specific conditions. Without control flow, a program would execute line-by-line, and the execution path would never change.

In Python, the primary control flow mechanisms are **conditional statements** and **loops.** Conditional statements, such as `if-else`, allow you to make decisions, whereas loops enable you to repeat tasks efficiently. Both tools are incredibly powerful when combined to solve real-world problems.

If-Else Statements: Making Decisions in Code

The `if-else` statement is one of the simplest yet most powerful tools for controlling the flow of your program. It allows you to execute a block of code only when a certain condition is true. If the condition is false, an optional block of code (the `else` part) can be executed.

Basic Syntax of If-Else Statements:

python

```python
if condition:
    # block of code if the condition is true
else:
    # block of code if the condition is false
```

The condition inside the `if` statement is an expression that evaluates to either `True` or `False`. If the condition is `True`, the code within the `if` block executes. If it's `False`, the code within the `else` block executes. This is ideal for situations where you need to choose between two possible actions.

For example, consider a program that checks whether a number is positive or negative:

python

```
num = -5

if num > 0:
    print("The number is positive.")
else:
    print("The number is negative.")
```

In this case, the program checks if the number `num` is greater than zero. Since `num` is -5, the `else` block will execute, printing "The number is negative."

Elif: Handling Multiple Conditions

What if you have more than two conditions to check? The `if-else` statement can be extended with `elif` (short for "else if") to handle multiple conditions.

```python
num = 10

if num > 0:
    print("The number is positive.")
elif num == 0:
    print("The number is zero.")
else:
    print("The number is negative.")
```

In this example, the program first checks if the number is positive. If it's not, it checks if the number is zero using the `elif` statement. If neither condition is true, the `else` block is executed.

Real-World Example of If-Else Statements

Consider a program that calculates a user's tax bracket based on their income:

```python
python

income = 45000

if income < 25000:
    tax_rate = 0.1  # 10%
elif income < 50000:
    tax_rate = 0.2  # 20%
else:
    tax_rate = 0.3  # 30%

print(f"Tax rate for an income of {income} is
{tax_rate*100}%")
```

This program checks the user's income against different thresholds and applies the appropriate tax rate. By using conditional statements, we can easily extend this logic to include more income brackets or change tax rates.

Loops: Repeating Tasks Efficiently

While `if-else` statements allow us to make decisions, loops allow us to repeat actions multiple times without having to write redundant code. In Python, there are two main types of loops: the **for loop** and the **while loop**. Both are used to repeat a block of code multiple times, but they are suited for different scenarios.

For Loops: Iterating Over Sequences

The `for` loop is used to iterate over a sequence (like a list, tuple, string, or range). It allows you to perform the same operation on each element in the sequence.

Basic Syntax of a For Loop:

```python
python
```

```
for item in sequence:
    # block of code to execute for each item in the
sequence
```

Let's say we have a list of numbers and we want to print each one:

```python
numbers = [1, 2, 3, 4, 5]

for num in numbers:
    print(num)
```

Here, the program loops through the list `numbers` and prints each number in turn. This is useful for situations where you need to process or modify each item in a collection.

Range: Iterating Over a Sequence of Numbers

You can also use the `range()` function in Python to generate a sequence of numbers. This is particularly useful when you don't have an existing list but need to repeat an action a certain number of times.

```python
for i in range(5):   # Iterates from 0 to 4
    print(i)
```

The `range()` function generates a sequence of numbers from the start value (0 by default) to the stop value (5, in this case). This is ideal for counting, performing repeated tasks a set number of times, or generating indices for other loops.

While Loops: Repeating as Long as a Condition is True

The `while` loop, on the other hand, repeats a block of code as long as a specified condition remains `True`. This loop is ideal when the number of iterations is not known in advance and depends on certain conditions being met.

Basic Syntax of a While Loop:

```python
while condition:
    # block of code to execute as long as the condition is true
```

Here's an example that repeatedly prompts a user for a number until they input a positive number:

```python
number = -1

while number <= 0:
    number = int(input("Please enter a positive number: "))

print(f"Thank you for entering {number}")
```

This program will keep asking the user for a positive number until they provide one. The loop continues running as long as `number <= 0`.

Breaking and Continuing in Loops

Sometimes, you may need to stop a loop early or skip the rest of the current iteration. This is where the `break` and `continue` statements come in.

- **Break:** The `break` statement is used to exit the loop immediately, regardless of the condition.

python

```
for i in range(10):
    if i == 5:
        break
    print(i)
```

In this example, the loop will stop when `i` equals 5, and the numbers `0` to `4` will be printed.

- **Continue:** The `continue` statement skips the rest of the current loop iteration and proceeds to the next iteration.

python

```
for i in range(10):
    if i % 2 == 0:
        continue
    print(i)
```

This program prints only odd numbers by skipping the even numbers using the `continue` statement.

List Comprehensions: A Compact and Pythonic Way to Work with Lists

List comprehensions provide a concise way to create lists in Python. They allow you to generate a new list by applying an expression to each item in an existing iterable, all within a single line of code. List comprehensions are not just more readable, but they are also more efficient than using traditional loops for creating lists.

Basic Syntax of a List Comprehension:
python

```
new_list = [expression for item in iterable if
condition]
```

- **Expression**: The value that you want to add to the new list.
- **Item**: The variable that takes each value in the iterable.
- **Iterable**: The collection you want to iterate over.
- **Condition**: An optional condition that filters the elements.

Example of a List Comprehension:

Let's say we want to create a list of squares for the numbers 0 through 9:

python

```
squares = [x ** 2 for x in range(10)]
print(squares)
```

This list comprehension generates a list of squares for each number in the range from 0 to 9. It's concise and readable.

List Comprehensions with Conditions:

You can also add a condition to your list comprehension to filter the items. For example, if you want to create a list of even squares only:

python

```
even_squares = [x ** 2 for x in range(10) if x % 2 ==
0]
print(even_squares)
```

In this case, the list comprehension filters out the odd numbers, only keeping the even ones.

Using List Comprehensions for More Complex Operations

List comprehensions can also be used for more complex transformations and operations. For example, let's say you want to convert a list of strings to uppercase:

python

```
words = ["hello", "world", "python"]
uppercase_words = [word.upper() for word in words]
print(uppercase_words)
```

This example demonstrates how list comprehensions can be used to apply functions or operations to each item in a list.

Practical Examples of Loops and Conditionals in Solving Coding Challenges

Now that we've covered the theory behind control flow, it's time to put it into practice. Let's look at some coding challenges where we can apply if-else statements, loops, and list comprehensions to solve problems efficiently.

Example 1: FizzBuzz

One of the most common coding challenges involves printing the numbers from 1 to 100, with the following conditions:

- For multiples of 3, print "Fizz".
- For multiples of 5, print "Buzz".
- For numbers that are multiples of both 3 and 5, print "FizzBuzz".

Here's how we can solve this using a `for` loop and `if-else` statements:

python

```python
for i in range(1, 101):
    if i % 3 == 0 and i % 5 == 0:
        print("FizzBuzz")
    elif i % 3 == 0:
        print("Fizz")
    elif i % 5 == 0:
        print("Buzz")
    else:
        print(i)
```

This program loops through the numbers from 1 to 100, checking the conditions for each one. It uses `if-else` statements to print the appropriate output.

Example 2: Generating Fibonacci Numbers

The Fibonacci sequence is a series of numbers where each number is the sum of the two preceding ones, starting from 0 and 1. The sequence goes: 0, 1, 1, 2, 3, 5, 8, 13, ...

Here's how to generate the first 10 Fibonacci numbers using a `while` loop:

python

```python
n = 10
fib = [0, 1]
while len(fib) < n:
    fib.append(fib[-1] + fib[-2])
print(fib)
```

In this example, the `while` loop continues until the length of the Fibonacci sequence reaches the desired count (`n`). It appends the sum of the last two numbers in the list to generate the next Fibonacci number.

Hands-On Example: Solve a Basic Problem Involving Loops and Conditional Statements

Let's implement a practical example that involves both loops and conditional statements. We'll create a program to track the grades of a class of students and categorize them based on their scores.

python

```python
# List of student names and their respective grades
students = [("Alice", 85), ("Bob", 78), ("Charlie",
92), ("David", 66), ("Eve", 55)]

# Function to categorize students based on their
grades
def categorize_grades(students):
    for name, grade in students:
        if grade >= 90:
            category = "A"
        elif grade >= 80:
            category = "B"
        elif grade >= 70:
            category = "C"
        elif grade >= 60:
            category = "D"
        else:
            category = "F"

        print(f"{name} scored {grade} and received a
grade of {category}")

# Call the function to categorize and display student
grades
categorize_grades(students)
```

In this program, we use a `for` loop to iterate over the list of students and their grades. For each student, we check their grade using an `if-else` chain and categorize them accordingly. This demonstrates how control flow and loops can be used together to solve a real-world problem.

Chapter 4: Functions: Writing Reusable and Efficient Code

Defining Functions and Understanding Function Scope

In any programming language, one of the most essential skills you can master is how to break down complex problems into smaller, manageable tasks. Python, being a high-level language that prioritizes readability and simplicity, provides a powerful tool to accomplish this: **functions**.

A **function** is essentially a block of code designed to perform a specific task. Once defined, a function can be executed (or "called") multiple times within a program, making your code cleaner, more efficient, and easier to maintain. Functions allow you to encapsulate logic, minimize redundancy, and enhance the reusability of your code.

In this chapter, we'll dive into the world of functions, exploring how to define them, how they work, and how to use them to organize and structure your programs effectively. We will also explore an important concept called **function scope**, which governs the visibility and lifetime of variables within a function.

What is a Function?

A function is a named block of code that performs a specific task. Once defined, you can call the function whenever needed, passing in data (called **arguments**) and receiving data back (called a **return value**).

In Python, functions are defined using the `def` keyword, followed by the function name, parentheses, and a colon. The code inside the function is indented to show that it belongs to that function.

Basic Syntax of a Function:

```python
def function_name(parameters):
    # code block
    return result
```

- **def**: This keyword is used to define a function in Python.
- **function_name**: The name of the function. It should be descriptive of what the function does.
- **parameters**: Optional input values that the function can take. Parameters allow the function to accept different inputs each time it is called.
- **return**: The value that the function outputs. The `return` statement sends data back to the caller.

A Simple Function Example

Let's start by defining a simple function that takes no parameters and returns a greeting:

```python
def greet():
    print("Hello, welcome to the world of Python!")
```

You can call this function like so:

```python
greet()
```

When you call `greet()`, Python will execute the code inside the function, printing "Hello, welcome to the world of Python!".

Functions allow you to encapsulate logic into a single unit of code that you can call whenever you need it, eliminating the need for repeating the same code throughout your program.

Function Parameters and Arguments

One of the key benefits of functions is the ability to pass **parameters**. Parameters are placeholders that allow functions to accept input values, making them more flexible.

For example, let's define a function that greets a specific person:

```python
def greet(name):
    print(f"Hello, {name}! Welcome to the world of
Python.")
```

Here, `name` is a parameter. When you call this function, you pass an argument that will replace `name`:

```python
greet("Alice")   # Output: Hello, Alice! Welcome to
the world of Python.
greet("Bob")     # Output: Hello, Bob! Welcome to the
world of Python.
```

The function now greets different people based on the arguments you provide when calling it.

Return Values: Sending Data Back from Functions

Functions can return values to the caller using the `return` keyword. This allows functions to compute results and send them back to where the function was called. The `return` statement also ends the function's execution.

Here's an example of a function that adds two numbers and returns the result:

```python
def add(a, b):
    return a + b
```

Now, when you call this function, you get a result:

```python
result = add(5, 3)   # result is now 8
print(result)   # Output: 8
```

By returning values, functions become even more useful, as they can be used as part of larger calculations or logic chains.

Function Scope: Understanding Local and Global Variables

When working with functions, it's important to understand **scope**. Scope refers to the region of your program where a variable is accessible. There are two main types of scope in Python:

1. **Local Scope**: Variables that are defined within a function are local to that function. They can only be accessed inside the function.
2. **Global Scope**: Variables that are defined outside of all functions are global and can be accessed anywhere in your program.

Let's look at an example:

python

```
def my_function():
    x = 10   # x is local to my_function
    print(x)

my_function()
print(x)   # This will raise an error because x is not
accessible outside the function
```

In this case, x is defined within the function and cannot be accessed outside of it. Python will raise an error if you try to print x outside the function because it's a local variable.

If you want to access or modify a global variable inside a function, you can use the `global` keyword. However, this should be done sparingly, as it can make your code harder to understand and maintain.

python

```
x = 5   # Global variable

def my_function():
    global x
    x = 10   # Modifies the global x

my_function()
print(x)   # Output: 10
```

In this case, the `global` keyword allows the function to modify the global variable x.

Breaking Down Complex Problems with Functions

One of the primary advantages of using functions is that they allow you to break down complex problems into smaller, more manageable tasks. Instead of writing one large block of code, you can divide your program into smaller pieces, each of which does one thing well. This makes your code easier to read, debug, and maintain.

Let's take a look at an example: Suppose you're tasked with creating a program that calculates the area of different shapes: rectangles, circles, and triangles.

Without functions, the code might look something like this:

```python
# Calculate the area of a rectangle
length = 5
width = 3
rectangle_area = length * width

# Calculate the area of a circle
import math
radius = 7
circle_area = math.pi * radius ** 2

# Calculate the area of a triangle
base = 4
height = 6
triangle_area = 0.5 * base * height

print("Rectangle area:", rectangle_area)
print("Circle area:", circle_area)
print("Triangle area:", triangle_area)
```

This works, but it's not very organized. If you need to calculate the area of these shapes in multiple parts of the program, you'll have to repeat the same code. Instead, we can break the problem down by creating a separate function for each shape's area calculation:

```python
import math

def rectangle_area(length, width):
    return length * width

def circle_area(radius):
    return math.pi * radius ** 2

def triangle_area(base, height):
    return 0.5 * base * height

# Now you can calculate the areas by calling the
functions:
print("Rectangle area:", rectangle_area(5, 3))
print("Circle area:", circle_area(7))
print("Triangle area:", triangle_area(4, 6))
```

By using functions, we've made our program more modular and reusable. If we need to calculate the area of a rectangle, circle, or triangle at a later point, we can simply call the corresponding function. We've broken down a potentially complex task into smaller, more manageable pieces of code.

Writing Clean, Reusable Functions

A key part of becoming a proficient programmer is learning how to write **clean, reusable functions**. Clean functions are not only easy to read and understand but also easy to maintain and debug. Reusable functions allow you to avoid code duplication, which makes your program easier to update and extend.

Here are some guidelines to help you write clean, reusable functions:

1. **Be Descriptive**: The function name should clearly describe what the function does. For example, a function that calculates the area of a rectangle should be named `calculate_rectangle_area`, not just `calculate`.
2. **Keep Functions Small**: A function should do one thing, and it should do it well. If a function is too long or complex, it's often a sign that it should be broken down into smaller functions.
3. **Use Parameters and Return Values**: Avoid using global variables inside functions. Instead, pass data to the function via parameters and return the result. This keeps your function isolated from the rest of the program, making it more reusable and easier to test.
4. **Avoid Side Effects**: Functions should ideally not change external states or have unintended consequences. Functions that modify global variables or perform I/O operations should be used cautiously, as they can lead to unexpected behavior.
5. **Document Your Functions**: Always add comments or docstrings to your functions. A docstring is a special kind of comment used to describe what the function does, its parameters, and its return value.

Here's an example of a well-documented function:

```python
def add(a, b):
```

```
"""
Adds two numbers together and returns the result.

Parameters:
a (int or float): The first number
b (int or float): The second number

Returns:
int or float: The sum of a and b
"""
return a + b
```

This makes the function easier to understand for others (or for yourself when you come back to it later). The docstring provides essential information about the function's purpose and usage.

Hands-On Example: Build a Calculator Program Using Functions

Now, let's take everything we've learned and put it into practice by building a simple calculator program using functions. The program will perform basic arithmetic operations like addition, subtraction, multiplication, and division.

Step 1: Define the Functions

We'll start by defining one function for each arithmetic operation. Each function will take two parameters, perform the corresponding operation, and return the result.

python

```python
def add(a, b):
    return a + b

def subtract(a, b):
    return a - b
```

```python
def multiply(a, b):
    return a * b

def divide(a, b):
    if b == 0:
        return "Cannot divide by zero"
    return a / b
```

Step 2: Create a Function to Display the Menu

Next, we'll create a function that displays a menu of available operations and allows the user to choose one.

python

```python
def display_menu():
    print("Simple Calculator")
    print("1. Add")
    print("2. Subtract")
    print("3. Multiply")
    print("4. Divide")
    print("5. Exit")
```

Step 3: Handle User Input

Now, we'll write the logic to prompt the user for input, call the appropriate function based on the user's choice, and display the result.

python

```python
def calculator():
    while True:
        display_menu()
        choice = input("Enter your choice (1/2/3/4/5): ")

        if choice == '1':
            a = float(input("Enter first number: "))
            b = float(input("Enter second number: "))
```

```
        print(f"Result: {add(a, b)}")
    elif choice == '2':
        a = float(input("Enter first number: "))
        b = float(input("Enter second number: "))
        print(f"Result: {subtract(a, b)}")
    elif choice == '3':
        a = float(input("Enter first number: "))
        b = float(input("Enter second number: "))
        print(f"Result: {multiply(a, b)}")
    elif choice == '4':
        a = float(input("Enter first number: "))
        b = float(input("Enter second number: "))
        print(f"Result: {divide(a, b)}")
    elif choice == '5':
        print("Exiting the calculator. Goodbye!")
        break
    else:
        print("Invalid choice. Please try
again.")
```

Step 4: Run the Program

To run the program, call the `calculator()` function:

```
python

calculator()
```

This simple calculator program demonstrates how functions can be used to modularize the code and break down the problem into smaller, manageable tasks. Each function performs a specific task (like adding two numbers), and the `calculator()` function ties everything together by prompting the user and displaying the results.

Chapter 5: Object-Oriented Programming (OOP) in Python

Key OOP Concepts: Classes, Objects, Inheritance, and Polymorphism

Object-Oriented Programming (OOP) is one of the most powerful paradigms in modern software development. It helps developers design complex programs that are modular, easy to understand, and maintain. If you've been programming for a while, you might have noticed that code sometimes becomes harder to manage as your projects grow. This is where OOP comes into play. It allows you to structure your code in a way that mirrors real-world interactions, making it easier to build, scale, and modify large applications.

In this chapter, we will explore the key concepts of OOP in Python, namely **classes**, **objects**, **inheritance**, and **polymorphism**. These concepts are foundational to OOP and will provide you with the tools you need to design more flexible and efficient programs. By the end of this chapter, you'll be able to create your own object-oriented systems and apply OOP principles to real-world problems.

What is Object-Oriented Programming (OOP)?

At its core, Object-Oriented Programming (OOP) is a programming model that organizes software design around **objects** and **classes**. It is based on several key principles that help in the organization and structure of your code, making it easier to scale and maintain.

- **Class**: A blueprint or template for creating objects. A class defines the attributes and behaviors that the objects created from the class will have.
- **Object**: An instance of a class. It is a concrete entity that has real values and is capable of performing operations defined in the class.
- **Inheritance**: A mechanism that allows a class to inherit attributes and methods from another class. This allows for code reuse and creates a hierarchical relationship between classes.
- **Polymorphism**: The ability to use a method in different ways depending on the context. It allows different classes to define the same method, but each can have its own implementation.

These principles enable you to model real-world objects and their behaviors in your code, creating a more intuitive and manageable system.

Classes and Objects: The Core of OOP

In OOP, a **class** is like a blueprint or a template, and an **object** is an instance of that class. Let's break it down further.

Defining a Class in Python

A class in Python is defined using the `class` keyword, followed by the name of the class. By convention, class names are written in **CamelCase** (e.g., `LibraryBook`). The body of the class contains the methods (functions) and attributes (variables) that define its behavior and properties.

Here's a simple example:

```python
class Dog:
    # Constructor method to initialize attributes
    def __init__(self, name, age):
        self.name = name   # Instance variable
        self.age = age     # Instance variable

    # Method to display information about the dog
    def bark(self):
        print(f"{self.name} says woof!")

    def get_age(self):
        return self.age
```

In this example, we define a class `Dog` with two attributes: `name` and `age`. The `__init__` method is the **constructor** method, which initializes the object's attributes when a new object is created. The `bark` method is an action that our `Dog` class can perform.

Creating an Object (Instantiating a Class)

Once you've defined a class, you can create an object of that class by calling the class name like a function, passing any necessary arguments to the constructor.

```python
# Creating a Dog object
my_dog = Dog("Buddy", 3)

# Accessing attributes and calling methods
print(my_dog.name)   # Output: Buddy
my_dog.bark()        # Output: Buddy says woof!
print(my_dog.get_age())  # Output: 3
```

Here, `my_dog` is an object (instance) of the `Dog` class. We can access its attributes (`name`, `age`) and invoke its methods (`bark`, `get_age`) just as we would with any real-world object.

Attributes and Methods

Attributes are variables that store data specific to an object, while methods define the actions or behaviors that an object can perform. In the `Dog` class example, `name` and `age` are attributes, and `bark()` and `get_age()` are methods.

- **Instance attributes** are specific to an instance of the class (e.g., `my_dog.name`).
- **Class attributes** are shared across all instances of the class (e.g., a `species` attribute that is the same for all `Dog` objects).

python

```python
class Dog:
    species = "Canis lupus familiaris"  # Class
attribute

    def __init__(self, name, age):
        self.name = name  # Instance attribute
        self.age = age    # Instance attribute

my_dog = Dog("Buddy", 3)
print(my_dog.species)  # Output: Canis lupus
familiaris
```

In this case, the `species` attribute is shared across all instances of the `Dog` class, while `name` and `age` are unique to each instance.

Inheritance: Building on Existing Classes

Inheritance allows one class to inherit the attributes and methods of another class. The class that is inherited from is called the **parent class** or **base class**, and the class that inherits is called the **child class** or **derived class**. This concept promotes code reuse and helps in building more complex systems by extending existing functionality.

Defining a Child Class

Here's an example of a child class inheriting from a parent class:

python

```python
class Animal:
    def __init__(self, name, species):
        self.name = name
        self.species = species

    def speak(self):
        print(f"{self.name} makes a sound")

class Dog(Animal):  # Dog inherits from Animal
    def __init__(self, name, age):
        super().__init__(name, "Dog")  # Calling the
constructor of the parent class
        self.age = age

    def speak(self):  # Overriding the speak method
        print(f"{self.name} barks")

class Cat(Animal):  # Cat inherits from Animal
    def __init__(self, name, age):
        super().__init__(name, "Cat")
        self.age = age

    def speak(self):  # Overriding the speak method
        print(f"{self.name} meows")
```

In this example, the `Dog` and `Cat` classes both inherit from the `Animal` class. The `super()` function is used to call the parent class's `__init__` method to initialize the shared attributes, and both `Dog` and `Cat` override the `speak()` method to provide their own implementations.

Using the Inherited Classes

Now, you can create objects of the child classes and access both inherited and overridden methods:

```python
python

dog = Dog("Buddy", 3)
cat = Cat("Whiskers", 2)

dog.speak()   # Output: Buddy barks
cat.speak()   # Output: Whiskers meows
```

By using inheritance, we can create specialized versions of the `Animal` class while still retaining the shared functionality.

Polymorphism: Same Method, Different Behavior

Polymorphism allows different classes to implement the same method in different ways. This is particularly useful when you have multiple objects that perform similar tasks but in different manners.

Polymorphism in Action

In the previous example, both `Dog` and `Cat` classes have a `speak` method. Even though both methods share the same name, they are implemented differently in each class. This is a classic example of **method overriding**, which is a type of polymorphism.

Here's another example using polymorphism to calculate the area of different shapes:

python

```python
class Shape:
    def area(self):
        pass   # This is a placeholder method to be overridden

class Circle(Shape):
    def __init__(self, radius):
        self.radius = radius

    def area(self):
        return 3.14 * self.radius ** 2

class Rectangle(Shape):
    def __init__(self, width, height):
        self.width = width
        self.height = height

    def area(self):
        return self.width * self.height
```

Now, you can create instances of different shape objects and call the `area()` method, which behaves differently depending on the type of object:

python

```python
circle = Circle(5)
rectangle = Rectangle(4, 6)

print(circle.area())    # Output: 78.5
print(rectangle.area())   # Output: 24
```

Here, `area()` is a polymorphic method because it behaves differently based on the type of object it's called on.

How OOP Helps in Structuring Large Programs and Making Code Modular

OOP is particularly effective when managing large codebases. It allows for a **modular design**, where each class can be developed, tested, and maintained independently. This modularity is key to scaling applications, enabling easy updates and bug fixes.

OOP helps in breaking down large, complex programs into smaller, more manageable chunks. By representing real-world entities as objects, you make the code more intuitive and easier to understand. Furthermore, the ability to reuse classes through inheritance reduces duplication, and polymorphism allows for flexibility in method implementation.

For example, in a library management system, you can represent books, members, and staff as separate classes. These classes can interact with each other without having to be tightly coupled, making the system easier to extend as new features are added.

Hands-On Example: Create a Simple Object-Oriented Class System for Managing a Library

Now that we've covered the theory behind OOP, let's apply what we've learned by building a simple **library management system**. This system will consist of classes for **Books**, **Members**, and **Library**.

Step 1: Define the Book Class

The Book class will represent a book in the library. Each book will have a title, author, and a status that indicates whether it's available or checked out.

python

```python
class Book:
    def __init__(self, title, author):
        self.title = title
        self.author = author
        self.available = True

    def check_out(self):
        if self.available:
            self.available = False
            print(f"'{self.title}' has been checked out.")
        else:
            print(f"'{self.title}' is already checked out.")

    def return_book(self):
        if not self.available:
            self.available = True
            print(f"'{self.title}' has been returned.")
        else:
            print(f"'{self.title}' was not checked out.")
```

Step 2: Define the Member Class

The Member class will represent a library member who can check out books. It will keep track of the books currently checked out by the member.

python

```python
class Member:
```

```python
    def __init__(self, name):
        self.name = name
        self.checked_out_books = []

    def check_out_book(self, book):
        if book.available:
            self.checked_out_books.append(book)
            book.check_out()
        else:
            print(f"Sorry, {self.name},
'{book.title}' is unavailable.")

    def return_book(self, book):
        if book in self.checked_out_books:
            self.checked_out_books.remove(book)
            book.return_book()
        else:
            print(f"{self.name} hasn't checked out
'{book.title}'.")
```

Step 3: Define the `Library` Class

The `Library` class will manage the collection of books and handle book checkouts and returns.

python

```python
class Library:
    def __init__(self):
        self.books = []

    def add_book(self, book):
        self.books.append(book)

    def list_books(self):
        for book in self.books:
            status = "Available" if book.available
else "Checked out"
            print(f"'{book.title}' by {book.author} -
{status}")
```

Step 4: Putting It All Together

Now, let's create an instance of the `Library`, add some books, create members, and perform checkouts and returns.

python

```python
library = Library()
book1 = Book("The Great Gatsby", "F. Scott
Fitzgerald")
book2 = Book("1984", "George Orwell")
library.add_book(book1)
library.add_book(book2)

member = Member("Alice")
member.check_out_book(book1)
library.list_books()

member.return_book(book1)
library.list_books()
```

Conclusion

In this chapter, we've explored the key principles of Object-Oriented Programming (OOP) in Python, including **classes**, **objects**, **inheritance**, and **polymorphism**. We've learned how to structure large programs and make code more modular, reusable, and maintainable by using OOP concepts. We also built a hands-on example—a simple library management system—to demonstrate how OOP can be applied in real-world applications.

By mastering OOP, you can build more scalable, flexible, and maintainable programs. Whether you're working on small scripts or large systems, OOP will help you keep your code organized and manageable, making it easier to scale and evolve your projects over time.

Chapter 6: Debugging and Error Handling Techniques

Common Python Errors and How to Handle Them

As you continue building Python applications, you will inevitably encounter errors. Whether you're a seasoned programmer or a beginner, errors are an unavoidable part of the coding process. What distinguishes a great programmer is not necessarily the ability to avoid errors, but the ability to **handle** and **fix** them efficiently. This chapter is designed to help you understand the types of errors you may encounter in Python, the mechanisms you can use to handle them, and the best strategies for debugging your code. Let's dive in.

What Are Errors?

An **error** in programming is any issue that causes a program to behave incorrectly, stop running, or fail to produce the expected result. In Python, errors are typically divided into two categories: **syntax errors** and **exceptions**.

1. **Syntax Errors:**
    - A syntax error occurs when Python can't interpret the code because it doesn't follow the correct syntax or structure. These are usually easy to spot because Python will point to the specific location of the error.
    - Example: A missing colon or parenthesis.

    ```python
    python
    ```

```
print("Hello, World!"  # Missing closing
parenthesis
```

The error message might look like this:

```
javascript
```

```
SyntaxError: unexpected EOF while parsing
```

Syntax errors prevent your program from running at all, which is why Python will flag them immediately.

2. **Exceptions**:
   o An exception is an error that occurs during the execution of a program. Unlike syntax errors, exceptions are raised when something goes wrong while the program is running. These errors can be caught and handled using Python's **exception handling** features.
   o Example: Dividing by zero.

```python
num1 = 10
num2 = 0
result = num1 / num2  # Division by zero error
```

The error message would be:

```
vbnet
```

```
ZeroDivisionError: division by zero
```

Types of Python Exceptions

There are many types of exceptions in Python, each representing a different kind of error. Here are a few common ones:

- **ZeroDivisionError**: Raised when attempting to divide by zero.
- **FileNotFoundError**: Raised when trying to access a file that doesn't exist.
- **ValueError**: Raised when a function receives an argument of the correct type but inappropriate value.
- **IndexError**: Raised when trying to access an index that is out of range in a sequence like a list or string.
- **KeyError**: Raised when trying to access a dictionary key that doesn't exist.
- **TypeError**: Raised when an operation is performed on an inappropriate data type.
- **NameError**: Raised when a local or global name is not found.

Using Try-Except Blocks to Manage Exceptions

Python provides an elegant way to handle exceptions using the `try-except` block. The basic idea is that you place the code that might cause an error inside the `try` block. If an error occurs, Python will jump to the `except` block, where you can handle the error in a controlled way.

Here's the basic syntax of the `try-except` block:

python

```python
try:
    # Code that may raise an exception
    risky_code()
except SomeException as e:
    # Code that handles the exception
    print(f"An error occurred: {e}")
```

In this structure:

- The **try block** contains the code you want to execute.
- The **except block** catches and handles the error if one occurs. The SomeException is the type of exception you expect, and e is the exception object that contains information about the error.

Example: Handling Division by Zero
python

```python
try:
    num1 = 10
    num2 = 0
    result = num1 / num2
except ZeroDivisionError as e:
    print(f"Error: {e}")
```

Output:

vbnet

```
Error: division by zero
```

In this case, Python detects the ZeroDivisionError and executes the code inside the except block instead of stopping the program.

Catching Multiple Exceptions

You can also catch multiple types of exceptions using multiple except blocks. For instance, if you're working with both FileNotFoundError and ZeroDivisionError, you can catch them separately:

python

```python
try:
    num1 = 10
    num2 = 0
```

```
    result = num1 / num2
except ZeroDivisionError:
    print("Error: Cannot divide by zero.")
except FileNotFoundError:
    print("Error: File not found.")
```

Alternatively, you can catch multiple exceptions in a single block:

python

```
try:
    num1 = 10
    num2 = 0
    result = num1 / num2
except (ZeroDivisionError, ValueError) as e:
    print(f"Error: {e}")
```

Using Else and Finally with Try-Except

Python also provides the `else` and `finally` blocks, which can be used in conjunction with `try-except` for better error handling and cleanup.

- **`else`**: If no exception is raised, the code inside the `else` block will run.
- **`finally`**: The code inside the `finally` block will always run, regardless of whether an exception is raised or not. It's useful for cleaning up resources, such as closing files or releasing network connections.

python

```
try:
    num1 = 10
    num2 = 5
    result = num1 / num2
except ZeroDivisionError:
    print("Cannot divide by zero!")
else:
```

```
    print(f"Result: {result}")
finally:
    print("Execution complete.")
```

Output:

```
makefile

Result: 2.0
Execution complete.
```

In this case, the `else` block runs because no error occurs, and the `finally` block executes regardless of the outcome.

Debugging Strategies and Python Tools for Error Tracking

While handling exceptions is an important part of writing reliable code, debugging is equally important. Debugging allows you to find and fix errors in your code before they cause issues in production.

Print Statements for Debugging

The simplest form of debugging is using **print statements** to understand what's happening inside your program. You can print variable values, intermediate results, and check flow paths.

```python
def divide_numbers(a, b):
    print(f"Dividing {a} by {b}")
    return a / b

result = divide_numbers(10, 2)
print(result)
```

However, print statements can clutter your code, and they are not always the most effective way to debug more complex programs.

Using Python's Built-In Debugger (pdb)

Python comes with a built-in debugger called pdb that allows you to step through your code, inspect variables, and execute commands interactively.

To use pdb, you insert the following line in your code where you want to start the debugger:

```python
import pdb; pdb.set_trace()
```

Once the program reaches this line, it will pause execution and enter the interactive debugging mode. You can then use commands like:

- n to step to the next line of code.
- c to continue execution.
- p to print the value of a variable.

Example:

```python
import pdb

def add_numbers(a, b):
    pdb.set_trace()  # Pauses execution here
    return a + b

result = add_numbers(5, 10)
print(result)
```

Using Logging for More Advanced Debugging

The `logging` module in Python provides a flexible way to log messages at different levels of severity (debug, info, warning, error, critical). It is more powerful than print statements because it gives you better control over what gets logged and where it gets output.

Here's an example of how to use logging:

```python
import logging

logging.basicConfig(level=logging.DEBUG)

def divide_numbers(a, b):
    logging.debug(f"Dividing {a} by {b}")
    if b == 0:
        logging.error("Division by zero!")
        return None
    return a / b

result = divide_numbers(10, 0)
```

In this example, a debug message is logged when the function is called, and an error message is logged if there's an attempt to divide by zero.

Third-Party Debugging Tools

For larger applications, you might want to use third-party debugging tools, such as:

- **Visual Studio Code**: A powerful IDE with integrated debugging support, allowing you to set breakpoints, step through code, and inspect variables.

- **PyCharm**: Another popular IDE with advanced debugging features, including remote debugging and support for testing frameworks.

Unit Testing for Debugging

Another way to catch errors early in development is by writing **unit tests**. Unit tests help you ensure that each part of your program works as expected, and they provide a safety net when making changes to your code. The `unittest` module in Python allows you to write and run tests to verify your code's behavior.

```python
import unittest

def add(a, b):
    return a + b

class TestAddFunction(unittest.TestCase):
    def test_add(self):
        self.assertEqual(add(2, 3), 5)
        self.assertEqual(add(-1, 1), 0)

if __name__ == '__main__':
    unittest.main()
```

In this example, `test_add()` checks whether the `add()` function behaves correctly with different inputs.

Hands-On Example: Debug a Broken Python Program and Handle Exceptions

Let's now put everything we've learned into practice by debugging a broken Python program and handling exceptions.

The Broken Program:

python

```
def calculate_area_of_circle(radius):
    pi = 3.14
    return pi * radius * radius

def get_user_input():
    radius = float(input("Enter the radius of the
circle: "))
    area = calculate_area_of_circle(radius)
    print(f"The area of the circle is: {area}")

get_user_input()
```

Issue #1: ValueError

What if the user enters something that's not a number? The program will crash with a ValueError if the user enters text instead of a numeric value. Let's handle that using a try-except block.

python

```
def get_user_input():
    try:
        radius = float(input("Enter the radius of the
circle: "))
        area = calculate_area_of_circle(radius)
        print(f"The area of the circle is: {area}")
    except ValueError:
        print("Invalid input! Please enter a numeric
value.")
```

Now, if the user enters something invalid, the program will handle the error gracefully by displaying a message instead of crashing.

Issue #2: Adding Logging

To help with debugging, let's add logging to our program. This will give us insight into the program's flow and data during runtime.

python

```python
import logging

logging.basicConfig(level=logging.DEBUG)

def calculate_area_of_circle(radius):
    logging.debug(f"Calculating area for radius: {radius}")
    pi = 3.14
    area = pi * radius * radius
    logging.debug(f"Calculated area: {area}")
    return area

def get_user_input():
    try:
        radius = float(input("Enter the radius of the circle: "))
        area = calculate_area_of_circle(radius)
        print(f"The area of the circle is: {area}")
    except ValueError:
        logging.error("Invalid input! Please enter a numeric value.")
        print("Invalid input! Please enter a numeric value.")
```

Now, when the program runs, it will log messages about the radius and the calculated area, helping you understand the flow of data.

Conclusion

In this chapter, we've covered the essential aspects of debugging and error handling in Python. We've discussed the common types of Python errors, including **syntax errors** and **exceptions,** and learned how to handle exceptions using `try-except` blocks. Additionally, we've explored debugging strategies, including using print statements, the built-in debugger (`pdb`), logging, and unit testing.

The goal of error handling and debugging is not only to fix problems but to create robust, fault-tolerant programs. By mastering these techniques, you'll be better equipped to handle unexpected situations in your code, and you'll be able to develop more reliable and maintainable Python applications.

Chapter 7: Working with Python Libraries and Modules

How to Use Python's Standard Library and Third-Party Modules

Python is one of the most versatile programming languages available today. Its ability to integrate easily with third-party libraries and its powerful standard library make it a great choice for almost any type of project. Whether you're working on data analysis, web development, automation, or even machine learning, Python's rich ecosystem of libraries and modules provides you with all the tools you need.

In this chapter, we will explore how to work with **Python's standard library**, as well as how to install and use **third-party modules**. By the end of this chapter, you'll have a solid understanding of how to extend Python's capabilities using both built-in libraries and external packages. Additionally, we'll walk through a practical example using Python's **os** library to manipulate files and directories.

What Are Libraries and Modules?

In Python, **modules** are simply files containing Python code that you can import into your own scripts. These files can contain functions, classes, and variables, and they allow you to organize and reuse code. Python's **standard library** is a collection of modules that come bundled with the Python installation. These modules provide functions and tools for a wide range of tasks like file I/O, regular expressions, networking, and more.

Libraries are collections of related modules, and they can either be part of the standard library or third-party libraries you install. Third-party libraries are created by developers outside of the Python core team and are often made available via package managers like **pip**.

Using Python's Standard Library

Python's standard library is vast and covers almost all areas of programming. It comes pre-installed with Python, so there's no need to install anything extra to use it. You can access any module in the standard library by importing it using the `import` statement.

Common Modules in the Standard Library

1. `math`: Provides mathematical functions like square root, trigonometric operations, and constants like `pi`.
2. `datetime`: Used for working with dates and times, such as calculating the difference between two dates or formatting dates for display.
3. `os`: Provides functions for interacting with the operating system, such as working with files and directories.
4. `sys`: Allows you to interact with the interpreter and manage command-line arguments and system-level functionality.
5. `random`: Used for generating random numbers and making random choices from a list or a sequence.
6. `re`: Provides support for regular expressions, allowing you to search and manipulate strings with complex patterns.

7. `json`: Used for working with JSON (JavaScript Object Notation), a popular format for storing and exchanging data.

Let's take a look at a few examples of how to use these built-in modules.

Example: Using `math` for Mathematical Operations

The `math` module contains many useful functions for working with numbers. Here's an example of using it to calculate the square root of a number and the sine of an angle:

python

```python
import math

# Calculate the square root of a number
num = 16
sqrt_num = math.sqrt(num)
print(f"Square root of {num} is {sqrt_num}")

# Calculate the sine of an angle (in radians)
angle = math.pi / 2  # 90 degrees in radians
sin_value = math.sin(angle)
print(f"Sine of {angle} radians is {sin_value}")
```

Output:

csharp

```
Square root of 16 is 4.0
Sine of 1.5707963267948966 radians is 1.0
```

Example: Using `datetime` for Date and Time Manipulation

The `datetime` module allows you to work with dates and times in a more Pythonic way. You can perform arithmetic on dates, compare them, and format them for display.

```python
python

import datetime

# Get the current date and time
now = datetime.datetime.now()
print(f"Current date and time: {now}")

# Create a specific date
specific_date = datetime.datetime(2022, 5, 17)
print(f"Specific date: {specific_date}")

# Calculate the difference between two dates
delta = now - specific_date
print(f"Difference between now and specific date:
{delta}")
```

Output:

```sql
sql

Current date and time: 2025-04-27 15:30:45.678453
Specific date: 2022-05-17 00:00:00
Difference between now and specific date: 1076 days,
15:30:45.678453
```

These examples show how the standard library can save you time and effort, allowing you to focus on solving the unique aspects of your project.

Using Third-Party Libraries

While Python's standard library is vast and covers a lot of use cases, sometimes you need additional functionality that isn't included by default. This is where third-party libraries come in. Python has a huge ecosystem of third-party libraries, available for almost any task you can imagine.

The most common way to install third-party libraries is through **pip**, Python's package installer. Pip allows you to download and install libraries from the **Python Package Index (PyPI)**, which hosts thousands of packages.

Installing a Library Using `pip`

To install a package using pip, open your terminal (or command prompt) and run the following command:

```bash
pip install package-name
```

For example, to install **NumPy**, a popular library for numerical computations, you would run:

```bash
pip install numpy
```

Once the package is installed, you can import it into your Python code:

```python
import numpy as np

# Create a NumPy array
arr = np.array([1, 2, 3, 4, 5])
print(arr)
```

Output:

```csharp
[1 2 3 4 5]
```

Exploring Popular Third-Party Libraries

1. **NumPy**: Used for numerical operations and working with large, multi-dimensional arrays and matrices. It's a powerful library for data analysis and scientific computing.
   - ○ Example: Using NumPy to calculate the mean of an array.

```python
import numpy as np

data = np.array([1, 2, 3, 4, 5])
mean = np.mean(data)
print(f"Mean of the data: {mean}")
```

Output:

```kotlin
Mean of the data: 3.0
```

2. **Pandas**: A library designed for data analysis and manipulation, providing powerful data structures like Series and DataFrame.
   - ○ Example: Using Pandas to load a CSV file and display the first few rows:

```python
import pandas as pd

# Load a CSV file into a DataFrame
df = pd.read_csv('data.csv')
print(df.head())   # Display the first few rows
of the DataFrame
```

3. **Matplotlib**: A plotting library used for creating static, animated, and interactive visualizations in Python.
   - Example: Using Matplotlib to plot a simple line graph:

```python
import matplotlib.pyplot as plt

# Data for plotting
x = [1, 2, 3, 4, 5]
y = [1, 4, 9, 16, 25]

plt.plot(x, y)
plt.xlabel('X-axis')
plt.ylabel('Y-axis')
plt.title('Simple Line Graph')
plt.show()
```

Output: A window will pop up displaying a simple line graph.

These libraries provide rich functionality and allow you to handle complex tasks with minimal code. Whether you're analyzing data with Pandas or visualizing it with Matplotlib, third-party libraries enable you to tackle problems more efficiently.

Managing Dependencies with `virtualenv`

When working with third-party libraries, you'll often encounter the issue of dependency management. Different projects may require different versions of the same library, which can lead to conflicts. This is where **virtual environments** come in.

A **virtual environment** is a self-contained directory that contains its own Python interpreter and libraries. This allows you to isolate dependencies for each project and avoid version conflicts.

To create a virtual environment, run:

```bash
python -m venv myenv
```

To activate the virtual environment:

- **On Windows**:

  ```bash
  myenv\Scripts\activate
  ```

- **On macOS/Linux**:

  ```bash
  source myenv/bin/activate
  ```

Once activated, you can install packages into the virtual environment without affecting other projects.

To deactivate the virtual environment when you're done, simply run:

```bash
deactivate
```

Using Python's os Library to Manipulate Files and Directories

One of the most useful libraries in Python's standard library is the **os** module. The os module provides a way to interact with the operating system and perform tasks such as manipulating files, directories, and paths.

Common Functions in the `os` Module

1. Working with Directories

- `os.mkdir(path)`: Creates a new directory at the specified path.
- `os.makedirs(path)`: Creates all intermediate directories if they don't exist.
- `os.chdir(path)`: Changes the current working directory.
- `os.listdir(path)`: Lists the files in the specified directory.

Example: Create a Directory and List Files
python

```python
import os

# Create a new directory
os.mkdir('new_folder')

# Change the current working directory
os.chdir('new_folder')

# List the files in the current directory
print(os.listdir())
```

2. Manipulating Files

- `os.rename(src, dst)`: Renames a file or directory.
- `os.remove(path)`: Deletes a file.
- `os.rmdir(path)`: Removes an empty directory.

Example: Rename a File
python

```
import os

# Create a test file
with open('test_file.txt', 'w') as f:
    f.write("This is a test file.")

# Rename the file
os.rename('test_file.txt', 'renamed_file.txt')

print("File renamed successfully.")
```

3. File Path Operations

- `os.path.join(path1, path2)`: Joins two or more paths together.
- `os.path.exists(path)`: Checks if a path exists.
- `os.path.isfile(path)`: Checks if a path is a file.
- `os.path.isdir(path)`: Checks if a path is a directory.

Example: Join Paths
python

```
import os

# Join paths
path = os.path.join('home', 'user', 'documents',
'file.txt')
print(path)  # Output: 'home/user/documents/file.txt'
```

Hands-On Example: Use Python's os Library to Manipulate Files and Directories

Let's build a simple Python program that interacts with the file system using the os library. The program will create a directory, add some files, and allow the user to delete files from that directory.

```python
python

import os

def create_directory(path):
    if not os.path.exists(path):
        os.mkdir(path)
        print(f"Directory '{path}' created.")
    else:
        print(f"Directory '{path}' already exists.")

def create_file(directory, filename, content):
    with open(os.path.join(directory, filename), 'w') as file:
        file.write(content)
        print(f"File '{filename}' created in '{directory}'.")

def delete_file(directory, filename):
    try:
        os.remove(os.path.join(directory, filename))
        print(f"File '{filename}' deleted.")
    except FileNotFoundError:
        print(f"File '{filename}' not found in '{directory}'.")

# Example usage
create_directory('test_folder')
create_file('test_folder', 'file1.txt', 'This is a test file.')
delete_file('test_folder', 'file1.txt')
```

This program demonstrates how to create directories, add files, and delete files using the os library. It's a simple example, but it shows how Python can be used to manage files and directories in a flexible and powerful way.

Conclusion

In this chapter, we've explored how to work with Python's standard library and third-party libraries to extend Python's functionality. The **standard library** provides a wide range of modules for handling everyday tasks, while **third-party libraries** like NumPy, Pandas, and Matplotlib allow you to work with data, visualize it, and perform complex computations with ease.

We also looked at the powerful `os` **module,** which allows you to manipulate files and directories. By mastering these libraries and tools, you'll be equipped to tackle any Python project with confidence.

Whether you're managing file systems, analyzing data, or building complex applications, Python's extensive ecosystem of libraries and modules makes it a great choice for any developer. By integrating these libraries into your code, you can save time, improve efficiency, and build more powerful and flexible applications.

Chapter 8: Solving Algorithms with Python

Introduction to Algorithms: Searching, Sorting, and Recursive Algorithms

In the world of computer science, **algorithms** are the foundation upon which most problems are solved. An algorithm is essentially a set of instructions that describe how to perform a task or solve a problem. The key idea behind algorithms is that they allow you to solve problems in a systematic, efficient, and repeatable way. Whether you're searching for a specific value in a large dataset, sorting a list of items, or dividing a problem into smaller sub-problems, algorithms are the key to achieving optimal performance.

In this chapter, we will explore three fundamental types of algorithms: **searching, sorting, and recursive algorithms**. These are essential concepts in computer science and will provide you with a solid foundation for tackling more complex problems. We'll also dive into how to analyze the **time complexity** and **space complexity** of algorithms to assess their efficiency.

By the end of this chapter, you'll be able to understand, implement, and optimize algorithms in Python, making you more efficient at solving computational problems.

Understanding and Implementing Basic Algorithms

Let's start by introducing the core types of algorithms and how we can implement them in Python.

1. Searching Algorithms

A **searching algorithm** is used to find a specific item in a collection of data. The two most common types of searching algorithms are **linear search** and **binary search**.

- **Linear Search**: This is the simplest searching algorithm. It works by checking each element in a list or array one by one until it finds the target element.

- o **Time Complexity**: O(n), where n is the number of elements in the list.
- o **Space Complexity**: O(1), since it doesn't require extra space beyond the list itself.

Implementation of Linear Search:

python

```python
def linear_search(arr, target):
    for i in range(len(arr)):
        if arr[i] == target:
            return i   # Return the index of the
found element
    return -1   # Return -1 if the target is not
found

# Example usage
arr = [10, 20, 30, 40, 50]
target = 30
result = linear_search(arr, target)
print(f"Element found at index {result}")   #
Output: Element found at index 2
```

- **Binary Search**: Binary search is much more efficient than linear search but requires the list to be **sorted**. It works by repeatedly dividing the search interval in half. If the target is smaller than the element at the middle of the list, it narrows the search to the left half, and if it's larger, the search continues on the right half.
  - o **Time Complexity**: O(log n), where n is the number of elements in the list.
  - o **Space Complexity**: O(1), since it only needs a constant amount of space.

Implementation of Binary Search:

python

```
def binary_search(arr, target):
    left, right = 0, len(arr) - 1
    while left <= right:
        mid = (left + right) // 2
        if arr[mid] == target:
            return mid  # Return the index of
the found element
        elif arr[mid] < target:
            left = mid + 1
        else:
            right = mid - 1
    return -1  # Return -1 if the target is not
found

# Example usage
arr = [10, 20, 30, 40, 50]
target = 30
result = binary_search(arr, target)
print(f"Element found at index {result}")  #
Output: Element found at index 2
```

2. Sorting Algorithms

Sorting algorithms are used to arrange the elements of a list or array in a specific order, typically in **ascending** or **descending** order. Sorting is a fundamental task in computer science because it allows for efficient searching, optimization, and better data presentation. There are several sorting algorithms, but we'll focus on two of the most popular ones: **Bubble Sort** and **Quick Sort**.

- **Bubble Sort**: This is a simple comparison-based sorting algorithm that works by repeatedly stepping through the list, comparing adjacent items and swapping them if they are in the wrong order. This process is repeated until the list is sorted.
  - **Time Complexity**: O(n^2), where n is the number of elements.

- Space Complexity: O(1), since it only requires a constant amount of space for swapping elements.

Implementation of Bubble Sort:

python

```python
def bubble_sort(arr):
    n = len(arr)
    for i in range(n):
        for j in range(0, n-i-1):
            if arr[j] > arr[j+1]:
                arr[j], arr[j+1] = arr[j+1], arr[j]  # Swap if elements are in the wrong order
    return arr

# Example usage
arr = [64, 34, 25, 12, 22, 11, 90]
sorted_arr = bubble_sort(arr)
print("Sorted array:", sorted_arr)   # Output:
Sorted array: [11, 12, 22, 25, 34, 64, 90]
```

- **Quick Sort:** Quick sort is an efficient, comparison-based sorting algorithm. It works by selecting a "pivot" element from the array and partitioning the other elements into two sub-arrays: those smaller than the pivot and those greater than the pivot. The sub-arrays are then sorted recursively.
  - **Time Complexity:** O(n log n) on average, O(n^2) in the worst case.
  - **Space Complexity:** O(log n) due to the recursive calls.

Implementation of Quick Sort:

python

```
def quick_sort(arr):
    if len(arr) <= 1:
        return arr
    pivot = arr[len(arr) // 2]   # Choosing the
middle element as pivot
    left = [x for x in arr if x < pivot]
    middle = [x for x in arr if x == pivot]
    right = [x for x in arr if x > pivot]
    return quick_sort(left) + middle +
quick_sort(right)

# Example usage
arr = [64, 34, 25, 12, 22, 11, 90]
sorted_arr = quick_sort(arr)
print("Sorted array:", sorted_arr)   # Output:
Sorted array: [11, 12, 22, 25, 34, 64, 90]
```

3. Recursive Algorithms

A **recursive algorithm** is one that solves a problem by solving smaller instances of the same problem. It breaks a large problem into sub-problems and calls itself with a smaller input. The recursion continues until it reaches a base case, which does not require further recursion.

A classic example of a recursive algorithm is the **factorial** calculation.

- **Factorial:** The factorial of a number n (denoted as n!) is the product of all positive integers from 1 to n. The factorial of 0 is defined as 1.

Implementation of Factorial Using Recursion:

python

```
def factorial(n):
    if n == 0:
        return 1
```

```
    else:
        return n * factorial(n - 1)

# Example usage
result = factorial(5)
print(f"Factorial of 5 is {result}")   # Output:
Factorial of 5 is 120
```

The recursive function `factorial(n)` calls itself with `n-1` until it reaches the base case, `n == 0`, where it stops and returns 1. Then, it "unwinds" the recursion and calculates the final result.

Time and Space Complexity Analysis

When working with algorithms, it is crucial to analyze their **time complexity** and **space complexity**. These two metrics help us understand how the algorithm performs as the input size grows.

- **Time Complexity**: Describes how the execution time of an algorithm grows as the input size increases. It's typically expressed using **Big O notation** (O(n), O(log n), O(n^2), etc.).
- **Space Complexity**: Describes how the memory usage of an algorithm grows as the input size increases.

Big O Notation: Big O notation is used to express the worst-case time or space complexity of an algorithm. It gives an upper bound on the growth of an algorithm as the input size increases.

For example:

- **O(1)**: Constant time complexity. The algorithm's performance does not depend on the input size.

- **O(n)**: Linear time complexity. The algorithm's performance grows linearly with the input size.
- **O(n^2)**: Quadratic time complexity. The algorithm's performance grows quadratically with the input size (common in algorithms with nested loops).

When analyzing sorting algorithms:

- **Bubble Sort** has a time complexity of O(n^2) because it involves nested loops.
- **Quick Sort** has an average time complexity of O(n log n), but in the worst case, it can be O(n^2).

Let's now look at a few common scenarios:

1. **Linear Search**:
   - Time Complexity: O(n) because we may need to examine every element in the list.
   - Space Complexity: O(1) because no extra space is needed.
2. **Quick Sort**:
   - Time Complexity: O(n log n) on average, O(n^2) in the worst case.
   - Space Complexity: O(log n) due to the recursion stack.
3. **Factorial**:
   - Time Complexity: O(n) because the function calls itself n times.
   - Space Complexity: O(n) due to the recursion stack.

By analyzing these complexities, you can decide which algorithm is more suitable for a given problem, especially when working with large datasets.

Hands-On Example: Implement a Sorting Algorithm (Quick Sort)

Let's walk through a hands-on example where we implement the **Quick Sort** algorithm. Quick Sort is a highly efficient sorting algorithm and is widely used in various applications. Here, we'll create a Python function that sorts a list of numbers using Quick Sort.

Step 1: The Quick Sort Algorithm

Quick Sort works by choosing a "pivot" element from the list and then partitioning the list into two sub-lists:

- Elements less than the pivot
- Elements greater than the pivot

We then recursively sort the two sub-lists. The base case for the recursion is when the list has zero or one element, which is already sorted.

Quick Sort Implementation:
python

```python
def quick_sort(arr):
    # Base case: a list with 0 or 1 elements is
already sorted
    if len(arr) <= 1:
        return arr
    # Recursive case: divide and conquer
    pivot = arr[len(arr) // 2]   # Choose the middle
element as the pivot
    left = [x for x in arr if x < pivot]  # Elements
smaller than the pivot
    middle = [x for x in arr if x == pivot]  #
Elements equal to the pivot
```

```
    right = [x for x in arr if x > pivot]   # Elements
greater than the pivot

    return quick_sort(left) + middle +
quick_sort(right)

# Example usage
arr = [64, 34, 25, 12, 22, 11, 90]
sorted_arr = quick_sort(arr)
print("Sorted array:", sorted_arr)   # Output: Sorted
array: [11, 12, 22, 25, 34, 64, 90]
```

Step 2: Explanation of the Code

- **Base Case**: If the list has only one element or is empty, we return the list because it is already sorted.
- **Pivot**: We choose the middle element of the list as the pivot, but you could choose other strategies for selecting the pivot.
- **Left, Middle, Right**: We divide the list into three sub-lists: the elements smaller than the pivot, the pivot itself, and the elements greater than the pivot.
- **Recursive Call**: We recursively call `quick_sort()` on the left and right sub-lists, and then concatenate the results with the middle list (the pivot).

Step 3: Analyzing the Time Complexity

Quick Sort is known for its efficient time complexity:

- **Best and Average Case**: O(n log n), where n is the number of elements in the list. This happens when the pivot is chosen well, and the list is divided into nearly equal parts.
- **Worst Case**: O(n^2), which occurs when the pivot is poorly chosen (e.g., the smallest or largest element).

This can be avoided with better pivot selection strategies like random pivoting.

Conclusion

In this chapter, we've explored fundamental algorithms like searching, sorting, and recursion. We've seen how to implement algorithms such as linear search, binary search, bubble sort, quick sort, and recursive algorithms like calculating the factorial. We also delved into time and space complexity analysis to evaluate the efficiency of algorithms, which is essential when working with large datasets.

The ability to understand and implement these algorithms efficiently in Python is crucial for solving a wide variety of problems in computer science and software engineering. As you continue your programming journey, mastering these basic algorithms will lay a solid foundation for tackling more complex challenges and optimizing your code for performance.

Chapter 9: Data Structures in Depth: Stacks, Queues, Linked Lists, and Trees

Advanced Data Structures: Stack, Queue, Linked List, and Tree

As we continue to deepen our understanding of Python and computer science, it's crucial to explore more advanced data structures. These structures—**Stacks, Queues, Linked Lists, and Trees**—are fundamental to efficient algorithm design and problem-solving. These data structures allow you to manage and organize data in ways that improve performance, enhance scalability, and make your programs more efficient.

In this chapter, we will take a deep dive into these data structures. We will learn how each structure works, explore their real-world applications, and understand how to implement them in Python. We will also focus on how to use these structures to solve common computational problems.

By the end of this chapter, you will be well-equipped with the knowledge of advanced data structures and their practical applications, enabling you to handle more complex problems and build more efficient solutions.

Understanding Advanced Data Structures

Let's begin by understanding how each of these data structures works and why they are important.

1. Stack: LIFO (Last In, First Out)

A **stack** is a linear data structure that follows the **LIFO (Last In, First Out)** principle. This means that the last element added to the stack will be the first one to be removed.

Imagine a stack of plates in a cafeteria: you add new plates to the top of the stack, and when you need a plate, you take the one from the top. The stack works in much the same way, where elements are **pushed** onto the top and **popped** from the top.

Key Operations:

- **Push**: Add an element to the top of the stack.
- **Pop**: Remove the element from the top of the stack.
- **Peek/Top**: View the top element without removing it.
- **IsEmpty**: Check if the stack is empty.

Real-World Applications:

- **Function Call Stack**: When a function is called in most programming languages, the function's details (such as local variables and the address to return to) are stored on a stack. This is managed by the operating system to keep track of function calls.
- **Undo Mechanism**: Applications like text editors or image editors use stacks to keep track of actions that can be undone.
- **Expression Evaluation**: Stacks are used in algorithms that evaluate expressions in postfix notation (Reverse Polish notation).

Implementation of a Stack in Python:

```python
python

class Stack:
    def __init__(self):
        self.stack = []

    def push(self, value):
        self.stack.append(value)

    def pop(self):
        if not self.is_empty():
            return self.stack.pop()
        else:
            return "Stack is empty"

    def peek(self):
        if not self.is_empty():
            return self.stack[-1]
        else:
            return "Stack is empty"

    def is_empty(self):
        return len(self.stack) == 0

    def size(self):
        return len(self.stack)

# Example usage:
stack = Stack()
stack.push(10)
stack.push(20)
print(stack.peek())      # Output: 20
print(stack.pop())       # Output: 20
print(stack.is_empty())  # Output: False
```

2. Queue: FIFO (First In, First Out)

A **queue** is a linear data structure that follows the **FIFO (First In, First Out)** principle. This means that the first element added to the queue will be the first one to be removed, just like waiting in line at a ticket counter.

Think of a queue like a line at a bank: the person who arrives first will be the first to be served, and others will follow in that order.

Key Operations:

- **Enqueue**: Add an element to the back of the queue.
- **Dequeue**: Remove the element from the front of the queue.
- **Front**: View the front element without removing it.
- **IsEmpty**: Check if the queue is empty.

Real-World Applications:

- **Print Queue**: Printers often use a queue to manage print jobs. The first job to enter the queue is the first job to be printed.
- **Task Scheduling**: Operating systems use queues to manage processes that are waiting to be executed.
- **Breadth-First Search (BFS)**: This is an algorithm that explores all neighbors at the present depth before moving on to nodes at the next depth level. A queue is an essential part of BFS.

Implementation of a Queue in Python:

```python
class Queue:
    def __init__(self):
        self.queue = []

    def enqueue(self, value):
        self.queue.append(value)

    def dequeue(self):
        if not self.is_empty():
```

```
            return self.queue.pop(0)
        else:
            return "Queue is empty"

    def front(self):
        if not self.is_empty():
            return self.queue[0]
        else:
            return "Queue is empty"

    def is_empty(self):
        return len(self.queue) == 0

    def size(self):
        return len(self.queue)

# Example usage:
queue = Queue()
queue.enqueue(10)
queue.enqueue(20)
print(queue.front())    # Output: 10
print(queue.dequeue())   # Output: 10
print(queue.is_empty())   # Output: False
```

3. Linked List: A Collection of Nodes

A **linked list** is a linear data structure that consists of a sequence of **nodes**, where each node contains two parts:

1. **Data**: The value or data stored in the node.
2. **Next**: A reference (or pointer) to the next node in the sequence.

Unlike arrays or lists, linked lists are **dynamic**, meaning they can grow or shrink in size as needed. They don't require a contiguous block of memory, unlike arrays, which makes them more flexible.

Key Operations:

- **Insert**: Add a node at a specific position in the list.
- **Delete**: Remove a node from the list.
- **Traverse**: Visit all the nodes in the list to retrieve their data.
- **Search**: Find a node with a specific value.

Real-World Applications:

- **Dynamic Memory Allocation**: Linked lists are used in applications where memory size is not known ahead of time and needs to be dynamically allocated.
- **Implementing Stacks and Queues**: Linked lists are often used to implement both stacks and queues because they allow efficient insertion and removal of elements.
- **Polynomial Representation**: Linked lists are used in mathematical applications, like representing polynomials, where each node holds a term of the polynomial.

Implementation of a Linked List in Python:

```python
class Node:
    def __init__(self, data):
        self.data = data
        self.next = None

class LinkedList:
    def __init__(self):
        self.head = None

    def insert(self, data):
        new_node = Node(data)
```

```
        new_node.next = self.head
        self.head = new_node

    def display(self):
        current = self.head
        while current:
            print(current.data, end=" -> ")
            current = current.next
        print("None")

    def delete(self, key):
        current = self.head
        if current and current.data == key:
            self.head = current.next
            current = None
            return
        prev = None
        while current and current.data != key:
            prev = current
            current = current.next
        if current is None:
            print("Node not found")
            return
        prev.next = current.next
        current = None

# Example usage:
ll = LinkedList()
ll.insert(10)
ll.insert(20)
ll.insert(30)
ll.display()   # Output: 30 -> 20 -> 10 -> None
ll.delete(20)
ll.display()   # Output: 30 -> 10 -> None
```

4. Trees: Hierarchical Data Structure

A **tree** is a hierarchical data structure that consists of nodes connected by edges. The topmost node is called the **root,** and each node can have **children**, which in turn can have their own children, forming a tree-like structure. Trees are particularly useful for representing hierarchical relationships such as organizational structures, file systems, or decision trees.

Key Operations:

- **Insert**: Add a node to the tree.
- **Search**: Find a node with a specific value.
- **Traverse**: Visit all the nodes in a tree (pre-order, in-order, post-order traversal).
- **Delete**: Remove a node from the tree.

Real-World Applications:

- **File Systems**: Operating systems use trees to organize directories and files in a hierarchical structure.
- **Decision Trees**: Used in machine learning and AI to make decisions based on a series of conditions.
- **Binary Search Trees (BST)**: A special type of tree used to store data in a way that allows for fast searching, insertion, and deletion operations.

Implementation of a Binary Tree in Python:

```python
class Node:
    def __init__(self, data):
        self.data = data
        self.left = None
        self.right = None

class BinaryTree:
    def __init__(self):
        self.root = None

    def insert(self, data):
        if not self.root:
            self.root = Node(data)
```

```
        else:
            self._insert_recursive(self.root, data)

    def _insert_recursive(self, node, data):
        if data < node.data:
            if node.left is None:
                node.left = Node(data)
            else:
                self._insert_recursive(node.left,
data)
        else:
            if node.right is None:
                node.right = Node(data)
            else:
                self._insert_recursive(node.right,
data)

    def display_inorder(self, node):
        if node:
            self.display_inorder(node.left)
            print(node.data, end=" ")
            self.display_inorder(node.right)

# Example usage:
bt = BinaryTree()
bt.insert(50)
bt.insert(30)
bt.insert(70)
bt.insert(20)
bt.insert(40)
bt.insert(60)
bt.insert(80)
bt.display_inorder(bt.root)   # Output: 20 30 40 50 60
70 80
```

Problem-Solving Strategies Using Advanced Data Structures

Now that we understand how these data structures work, let's discuss how to solve problems effectively by choosing the right data structure. Each data structure serves a specific purpose, and knowing when and how to use them can significantly improve your problem-solving efficiency.

When to Use Stacks

Stacks are particularly useful when you need to handle tasks in a **reverse order**, such as:

- **Expression evaluation** (e.g., evaluating postfix or prefix expressions).
- **Function calls** (the call stack in recursion or function calls).
- **Undo operations** in applications, where the last operation must be reversed first.

When to Use Queues

Queues are ideal for handling tasks in a **first-come, first-served order**:

- **Scheduling tasks**: For example, print jobs are processed in the order they are received.
- **Breadth-First Search (BFS)**: In graph traversal, BFS explores nodes level by level, which can be efficiently implemented using a queue.
- **Event-driven simulations**: Like handling requests or processing jobs in real-time.

When to Use Linked Lists

Linked lists are useful when you need a **dynamic structure** that allows for efficient insertion and deletion:

- **Memory-efficient structures**: Linked lists don't require contiguous memory, unlike arrays, and are more flexible in size.
- **Implementing stacks and queues**: You can use linked lists to build these data structures efficiently.
- **Dynamic lists**: When the list size changes frequently, linked lists offer better performance than arrays.

When to Use Trees

Trees are perfect for hierarchical relationships, and when you need fast searching, sorting, or traversal:

- **File systems**: Directories and files are stored in a tree structure.
- **Databases**: Search trees like B-trees or AVL trees are used in databases for efficient searching.
- **Decision-making models**: In machine learning, trees (like decision trees) help in making decisions based on conditions.

Hands-On Example: Build a Stack Data Structure and Solve a Problem Using It

Let's build a **stack** from scratch and use it to solve a practical problem: reversing a string.

Step 1: Implementing a Stack
python

```python
class Stack:
    def __init__(self):
        self.stack = []

    def push(self, value):
        self.stack.append(value)
```

```python
    def pop(self):
        if not self.is_empty():
            return self.stack.pop()
        return None

    def peek(self):
        if not self.is_empty():
            return self.stack[-1]
        return None

    def is_empty(self):
        return len(self.stack) == 0

# Example usage:
stack = Stack()
stack.push("H")
stack.push("e")
stack.push("l")
stack.push("l")
stack.push("o")

# Reversing the string using the stack
reversed_string = ""
while not stack.is_empty():
    reversed_string += stack.pop()

print("Reversed String:", reversed_string)   # Output:
"olleH"
```

Step 2: Explanation

1. We first implement a stack using a class. The stack uses a list to hold elements, and we define the basic operations (push, pop, peek, and is_empty).
2. To reverse a string, we push each character of the string onto the stack.
3. We then pop each character off the stack and concatenate it to form the reversed string. Since the stack follows the LIFO principle, this reverses the order of characters.

This problem illustrates how stacks can be used to manage data in a reverse order, a common scenario in many real-world applications.

Conclusion

In this chapter, we've explored **advanced data structures** such as **stacks, queues, linked lists**, and **trees**. These data structures are the building blocks for solving more complex problems in Python and computer science in general. We've learned about the key operations for each structure and discussed their real-world applications.

We also covered problem-solving strategies for when to use these data structures, depending on the specific needs of the task. By mastering these advanced structures, you'll be well-equipped to solve a wide variety of problems efficiently.

In the hands-on example, we built a stack data structure and used it to solve a simple yet practical problem: reversing a string. This is just one of many applications of stacks, and the concepts learned here can be applied to more complex algorithms and real-world scenarios.

As you continue to grow as a programmer, understanding when and how to use these advanced data structures will be crucial to optimizing the performance and scalability of your solutions.

Chapter 10: Working with Databases and SQL in Python

How to Interact with Databases Using Python

Databases play an essential role in managing and storing large amounts of data for applications. Whether you're building a simple website, a mobile app, or a complex enterprise application, you'll likely need a way to store and retrieve data efficiently. **SQL** (Structured Query Language) is the standard language used to interact with relational databases, and Python provides powerful tools for connecting to and managing databases.

In this chapter, we will explore how Python can be used to interact with databases, focusing specifically on Python's **sqlite3 module**—a built-in library that allows you to work with **SQLite** databases. We will also introduce the basics of **SQL**, the language used for querying and manipulating data in a relational database, and demonstrate how you can build a simple **inventory management system** using SQLite and Python.

By the end of this chapter, you will have a solid understanding of how databases work, how to use SQL queries to interact with a database, and how to apply these concepts in a practical example.

What is a Database?

A **database** is a collection of data organized in a structured way so that it can be easily accessed, managed, and updated. Relational databases, such as SQLite, store data in tables, which consist of rows and columns. Each column represents a field (attribute), and each row represents a record (entry) in the database. This structure makes it easy to perform operations like querying, updating, and deleting data.

SQL (Structured Query Language) is the standard language for interacting with relational databases. It provides commands to perform tasks like inserting new data, updating existing data, and retrieving data using queries.

Types of Databases

There are many types of databases, but the most common are:

- **Relational Databases**: These databases organize data into tables with rows and columns. Examples include **MySQL, PostgreSQL, Oracle**, and **SQLite**.
- **NoSQL Databases**: These databases store data in formats other than tables, such as documents, key-value pairs, or graphs. Examples include **MongoDB, Cassandra**, and **Redis**.

For this chapter, we'll focus on **SQLite**, a lightweight, self-contained relational database that is built into Python's standard library through the **sqlite3 module**.

SQLite and the sqlite3 Module in Python

SQLite is a serverless, zero-configuration database engine that stores data in a single file. It is widely used for small to medium-sized applications due to its simplicity and ease of setup. Unlike other database systems like MySQL or PostgreSQL, SQLite doesn't require a separate server process. It's embedded into the application, making it an excellent choice for local storage and development.

The **sqlite3 module** in Python provides a simple interface to interact with SQLite databases. It allows you to execute SQL commands, manage database connections, and retrieve query results—all from within your Python code.

How to Use sqlite3 in Python

1. **Connecting to a Database**: To interact with an SQLite database, you first need to establish a connection. If the database file does not exist, SQLite will automatically create it.

   ```python
   import sqlite3

   # Connect to a database (or create it if it
   doesn't exist)
   conn = sqlite3.connect('example.db')
   ```

   In the above code, `'example.db'` is the name of the SQLite database file. If this file doesn't exist, SQLite will create it.

2. **Creating a Cursor**: A **cursor** is used to execute SQL queries and retrieve results. Once you have a connection, you can create a cursor object.

   ```python
   cursor = conn.cursor()
   ```

3. **Executing SQL Commands**: The `cursor.execute()` method allows you to execute SQL queries, such as creating tables, inserting data, or querying records.

   ```python
   ```

```
cursor.execute('CREATE TABLE IF NOT EXISTS
users (id INTEGER PRIMARY KEY, name TEXT, age
INTEGER)')
```

4. **Committing Changes**: After making changes to the database (like inserting, updating, or deleting data), you need to **commit** the transaction to save it.

```python
python
```

```
conn.commit()
```

5. **Closing the Connection**: After you're done with database operations, it's good practice to close the connection.

```python
python
```

```
conn.close()
```

Introduction to SQL and Database Management

SQL (Structured Query Language) is a standardized programming language used to manage and manipulate data in relational databases. It's divided into several types of commands:

1. **Data Definition Language (DDL)**:
    - `CREATE`: Used to create tables, views, indexes, etc.
    - `ALTER`: Used to modify an existing database object.
    - `DROP`: Used to delete database objects.
2. **Data Manipulation Language (DML)**:
    - `SELECT`: Used to query data from a table.
    - `INSERT`: Used to insert data into a table.
    - `UPDATE`: Used to modify existing data in a table.

- ○ DELETE: Used to remove data from a table.
3. **Data Control Language (DCL):**
    - ○ GRANT: Used to give a user access privileges.
    - ○ REVOKE: Used to remove access privileges.

Basic SQL Commands

Let's start with some of the most common SQL commands:

1. **CREATE TABLE**: To create a new table in the database.

    ```sql
    CREATE TABLE users (
        id INTEGER PRIMARY KEY,
        name TEXT,
        age INTEGER
    );
    ```

2. **INSERT INTO**: To insert data into a table.

    ```sql
    INSERT INTO users (name, age) VALUES ('Alice',
    30);
    ```

3. **SELECT**: To retrieve data from a table.

    ```sql
    SELECT * FROM users;
    ```

4. **UPDATE**: To modify existing records in a table.

    ```sql
    UPDATE users SET age = 31 WHERE name = 'Alice';
    ```

5. **DELETE**: To delete records from a table.

```sql
sql

DELETE FROM users WHERE name = 'Alice';
```

These commands are the building blocks of working with databases. Now that we have a general understanding of SQL, let's move on to building a practical example.

Hands-On Example: Build a Simple Inventory Management System with SQLite

Let's build a simple **inventory management system** where we can add items to an inventory, update their details, and view the inventory. This example will use Python's `sqlite3` module to interact with the database and SQL commands to manipulate the data.

Step 1: Design the Database

For our inventory system, we'll need a table that holds the inventory items. Each item will have the following attributes:

- `id`: A unique identifier for each item (Primary Key).
- `name`: The name of the item.
- `quantity`: The quantity of the item in stock.
- `price`: The price of a single unit.

We will start by creating the database and the table.

```python
python

import sqlite3
```

```
# Connect to the database (it will be created if it
doesn't exist)
conn = sqlite3.connect('inventory.db')
cursor = conn.cursor()

# Create the inventory table
cursor.execute('''CREATE TABLE IF NOT EXISTS
inventory (
                  id INTEGER PRIMARY KEY
AUTOINCREMENT,
                  name TEXT,
                  quantity INTEGER,
                  price REAL)''')

# Commit the changes and close the connection
conn.commit()
```

Step 2: Adding Items to the Inventory

Next, we will create a function to add new items to the inventory. This function will take the item name, quantity, and price as parameters and insert them into the database.

python

```
def add_item(name, quantity, price):
    conn = sqlite3.connect('inventory.db')
    cursor = conn.cursor()

    # Insert a new item into the inventory
    cursor.execute('''INSERT INTO inventory (name,
quantity, price)
                      VALUES (?, ?, ?)''', (name,
quantity, price))

    conn.commit()
    conn.close()

# Example usage:
add_item('Laptop', 10, 999.99)
add_item('Smartphone', 20, 499.99)
```

Step 3: Viewing the Inventory

Now let's create a function that retrieves all the items in the inventory and displays them.

python

```python
def view_inventory():
    conn = sqlite3.connect('inventory.db')
    cursor = conn.cursor()

    # Select all items from the inventory
    cursor.execute('SELECT * FROM inventory')
    items = cursor.fetchall()

    # Print the items in a user-friendly format
    for item in items:
        print(f"ID: {item[0]}, Name: {item[1]},
Quantity: {item[2]}, Price: ${item[3]:.2f}")

    conn.close()

# Example usage:
view_inventory()
```

Output:

yaml

```yaml
ID: 1, Name: Laptop, Quantity: 10, Price: $999.99
ID: 2, Name: Smartphone, Quantity: 20, Price: $499.99
```

Step 4: Updating Inventory Items

Let's now create a function that allows us to update the quantity of an item in the inventory. This function will take the item ID and the new quantity as parameters.

python

```python
def update_quantity(item_id, new_quantity):
```

```
conn = sqlite3.connect('inventory.db')
cursor = conn.cursor()

# Update the quantity of the item
cursor.execute('''UPDATE inventory
                  SET quantity = ?
                  WHERE id = ?''', (new_quantity,
item_id))

conn.commit()
conn.close()

# Example usage:
update_quantity(1, 15)   # Update the quantity of the
item with ID 1
view_inventory()
```

Output:

yaml

```
ID: 1, Name: Laptop, Quantity: 15, Price: $999.99
ID: 2, Name: Smartphone, Quantity: 20, Price: $499.99
```

Step 5: Deleting Items from the Inventory

Finally, let's create a function that allows us to delete an item from the inventory by its ID.

python

```
def delete_item(item_id):
    conn = sqlite3.connect('inventory.db')
    cursor = conn.cursor()

    # Delete the item from the inventory
    cursor.execute('''DELETE FROM inventory WHERE id
= ?''', (item_id,))

    conn.commit()
    conn.close()

# Example usage:
```

```
delete_item(2)   # Delete the item with ID 2
view_inventory()
```

Output:

```
yaml

ID: 1, Name: Laptop, Quantity: 15, Price: $999.99
```

Conclusion

In this chapter, we explored how to interact with databases using Python's built-in **sqlite3 module**. We discussed the basics of databases, how to connect to an SQLite database, execute SQL commands to create tables, insert, update, and delete data, and how to retrieve and display data in Python.

We also walked through the process of building a **simple inventory management system** using SQLite. This hands-on example helped demonstrate how to use Python to manage data in a real-world application.

By now, you should have a solid understanding of how to:

- Create and manage SQLite databases.
- Use SQL to interact with data.
- Build simple applications that store and manipulate data using Python.

Mastering databases and SQL is essential for working on real-world applications, especially when dealing with large datasets, and this knowledge will serve as a foundation for more advanced database systems and operations.

Chapter 11: File Handling and Data Parsing

Reading from and Writing to Files in Python

File handling is a core aspect of many programming tasks. Whether you're building a system to log data, process user input, or manage configuration files, you'll often need to work with files. In Python, file handling is straightforward, yet powerful enough to handle a wide range of file-related operations, from simple text file manipulation to complex data processing tasks.

In this chapter, we will explore how to read from and write to files in Python. We will discuss the **different modes** available for opening files, how to efficiently manage file input and output (I/O), and techniques for working with large datasets, such as **CSV** and **JSON** files. By the end of this chapter, you will have the skills needed to handle file operations in Python, including parsing structured data like CSV and JSON files, all while keeping your code efficient and scalable.

What is File Handling?

In programming, **file handling** refers to the operations performed to read from and write to files stored on a computer's file system. Files can be used to store data persistently, which means even if the program ends or the computer is restarted, the data can still be retrieved from the file. Python provides simple functions to work with files, allowing you to perform operations like:

- Opening and closing files
- Reading data from files
- Writing data to files
- Modifying file contents
- Managing file paths and directories

Python provides a built-in function called `open()` for opening files, and this function returns a file object that can be used to read, write, or modify the file's contents. Once you're done working with the file, it's important to close it to free up system resources using the `close()` method.

Opening a File

To open a file, use Python's built-in `open()` function. This function requires two arguments:

1. The **file name** (or path to the file).
2. The **mode** in which the file should be opened.

Basic Syntax:

```python
file = open('file.txt', 'mode')
```

Here are some common modes used when opening a file:

- `'r'`: Read (default mode). Opens the file for reading.
- `'w'`: Write. Opens the file for writing, creating the file if it doesn't exist.
- `'a'`: Append. Opens the file for writing, but appends data to the end of the file if it exists.
- `'b'`: Binary. Used in combination with other modes for binary files (e.g., `'rb'` or `'wb'`).

- `'x'`: Exclusive creation. Creates a new file, but raises an error if the file already exists.

Let's look at how to use these modes:

```python
# Open a file for reading
file = open('file.txt', 'r')

# Open a file for writing
file = open('file.txt', 'w')

# Open a file for appending
file = open('file.txt', 'a')
```

Reading from Files

There are several ways to read data from a file in Python:

1. **Read the entire content** using `read()`:

   ```python
   file = open('file.txt', 'r')
   content = file.read()
   print(content)
   file.close()
   ```

2. **Read line by line** using `readline()`:

   ```python
   file = open('file.txt', 'r')
   line = file.readline()
   while line:
       print(line, end='')   # end='' prevents extra newline
       line = file.readline()
   file.close()
   ```

3. **Read all lines into a list** using `readlines()`:

```python
file = open('file.txt', 'r')
lines = file.readlines()
for line in lines:
    print(line, end='')
file.close()
```

Writing to Files

When writing to a file, you can either overwrite the contents or append data to an existing file. Here's how you can use the different modes:

1. **Write data to a file** using `write()`:

```python
file = open('file.txt', 'w')
file.write("Hello, World!\n")
file.write("Welcome to file handling in
Python.")
file.close()
```

2. **Append data to a file** using `write()` in append mode:

```python
file = open('file.txt', 'a')
file.write("\nThis is an appended line.")
file.close()
```

3. **Write multiple lines** using `writelines()`:

```python
file = open('file.txt', 'w')
```

```
lines = ["First line\n", "Second line\n",
"Third line\n"]
file.writelines(lines)
file.close()
```

Using `with` Statement for File Handling

Instead of manually opening and closing files, Python provides a more elegant way to handle files using the `with` statement. This automatically handles closing the file when the block of code is finished, even if an error occurs.

```
python
```

```python
with open('file.txt', 'r') as file:
    content = file.read()
    print(content)
# No need to call file.close(), it's automatically
handled.
```

Techniques for Working with Large Datasets and Parsing JSON or CSV Files

Working with large datasets requires more efficient ways of reading and writing data, especially when dealing with structured data formats like **CSV** and **JSON**. Python provides built-in libraries to handle these formats, and understanding how to work with them is crucial for data science, web development, and other applications that involve large-scale data.

Working with CSV Files

CSV (Comma-Separated Values) files are a popular format for storing tabular data, such as spreadsheets or database exports. Python's `csv` module makes it easy to read from and write to CSV files.

Reading a CSV File:

```python
python

import csv

with open('data.csv', 'r') as file:
    csv_reader = csv.reader(file)
    for row in csv_reader:
        print(row)
```

This will print each row from the CSV file as a list of values.

Writing to a CSV File:

```python
python

import csv

data = [["Name", "Age", "City"], ["Alice", 30, "New York"], ["Bob", 25, "Los Angeles"]]

with open('output.csv', 'w', newline='') as file:
    csv_writer = csv.writer(file)
    csv_writer.writerows(data)
```

Working with CSV Dictionaries: If you prefer to work with CSV data as dictionaries (where each row is a dictionary with field names as keys), use `csv.DictReader()` and `csv.DictWriter()`.

Reading a CSV as a Dictionary:

```python
python

import csv

with open('data.csv', 'r') as file:
    csv_reader = csv.DictReader(file)
    for row in csv_reader:
```

```
    print(row)
```

Writing to a CSV as a Dictionary:

```
python

import csv

data = [
    {"Name": "Alice", "Age": 30, "City": "New York"},
    {"Name": "Bob", "Age": 25, "City": "Los Angeles"}
]

with open('output.csv', 'w', newline='') as file:
    fieldnames = ["Name", "Age", "City"]
    csv_writer = csv.DictWriter(file,
fieldnames=fieldnames)
    csv_writer.writeheader()
    csv_writer.writerows(data)
```

Working with JSON Files

JSON (JavaScript Object Notation) is a lightweight data interchange format that is easy to read and write. Python's built-in json module provides methods to parse and manipulate JSON data.

Reading JSON Data:

```
python

import json

with open('data.json', 'r') as file:
    data = json.load(file)  # Parses the JSON data
into a Python dictionary
    print(data)
```

Writing JSON Data:

```
python
```

```python
import json

data = {"name": "Alice", "age": 30, "city": "New
York"}

with open('output.json', 'w') as file:
    json.dump(data, file, indent=4)  # Write JSON
data with indentation
```

How to Handle File I/O Efficiently

When working with large datasets or handling file I/O operations frequently, efficiency becomes critical. Here are some tips to improve the performance of your file handling operations.

1. Use Buffered I/O for Large Files

When working with large files, reading or writing the file in small chunks (buffered I/O) can be more efficient than reading or writing the entire file at once.

python

```python
with open('large_file.txt', 'r') as file:
    for line in file:
        # Process each line here
        print(line.strip())
```

2. Reading Files Line by Line

For large text files, reading the file line by line is often more memory-efficient than reading the entire file into memory at once.

python

```python
with open('large_file.txt', 'r') as file:
    for line in file:
```

```
            # Process each line
            print(line.strip())
```

3. Writing Files in Chunks

When writing large data to files, it's often more efficient to write the data in chunks rather than writing everything at once.

python

```
data = ["line1\n", "line2\n", "line3\n"]
with open('output.txt', 'w') as file:
    for line in data:
        file.write(line)
```

4. Using Memory-Mapped Files

For very large files that you need to read and modify efficiently, Python's mmap module allows you to memory-map files, providing access to file contents without reading them entirely into memory.

python

```
import mmap

with open('large_file.txt', 'r+') as file:
    # Memory-map the file, size 0 means the entire
file
    mmapped_file = mmap.mmap(file.fileno(), 0)
    print(mmapped_file[:10])  # Read the first 10
bytes
    mmapped_file.close()
```

Hands-On Example: Write a Python Program to Read and Write Customer Data to a File

Let's build a **customer management system** that reads and writes customer data to a text file. Each customer will have a name, email, and phone number, and we'll implement functionality to add new customers, list all customers, and save the customer data to a file.

Step 1: Define the Customer Class

We'll define a class to represent a customer.

python

```python
class Customer:
    def __init__(self, name, email, phone):
        self.name = name
        self.email = email
        self.phone = phone

    def __str__(self):
        return f"Name: {self.name}, Email: {self.email}, Phone: {self.phone}"
```

Step 2: Save Customers to a File

Now, let's write a function to save customer data to a file.

python

```python
def save_customers(customers,
filename="customers.txt"):
    with open(filename, 'w') as file:
        for customer in customers:

file.write(f"{customer.name},{customer.email},{customer.phone}\n")
```

Step 3: Load Customers from a File

We also need a function to load customer data from the file.

python

```python
def load_customers(filename="customers.txt"):
```

```
    customers = []
    try:
        with open(filename, 'r') as file:
            for line in file:
                name, email, phone =
line.strip().split(',')
                customers.append(Customer(name,
email, phone))
    except FileNotFoundError:
        print(f"{filename} not found.")
    return customers
```

Step 4: Add and Display Customers

Let's create a function to add a new customer and display all customers.

python

```python
def add_customer(customers, name, email, phone):
    customer = Customer(name, email, phone)
    customers.append(customer)

def display_customers(customers):
    for customer in customers:
        print(customer)
```

Step 5: Putting It All Together

Now, we can put everything together in a simple main function that adds customers, saves them to a file, and loads the customers back from the file.

python

```python
def main():
    customers = load_customers()

    # Add new customers
    add_customer(customers, "Alice",
"alice@example.com", "123-456-7890")
```

```
    add_customer(customers, "Bob", "bob@example.com",
"987-654-3210")

    # Display all customers
    print("All Customers:")
    display_customers(customers)

    # Save the customers to a file
    save_customers(customers)

    print("Customer data saved.")

# Example usage
main()
```

This program will:

1. Load existing customers from the file (if available).
2. Add new customers.
3. Display the customer list.
4. Save the updated customer data back to the file.

Conclusion

In this chapter, we've covered how to read from and write to files in Python, techniques for working with large datasets, and how to handle file I/O efficiently. We also explored how to parse **CSV** and **JSON** files—two common formats used for data storage and exchange.

Using Python's built-in file handling functions and libraries like csv and json, you can efficiently manage data, even when dealing with large datasets. The hands-on example we created—a simple customer management system—demonstrates how to implement file handling and data parsing in a practical scenario.

With the knowledge gained in this chapter, you are now equipped to handle various file I/O operations, efficiently work with large datasets, and parse structured data formats like CSV and JSON in Python. Whether you are building data-driven applications, processing logs, or managing configuration files, file handling is a crucial skill for every developer.

Chapter 12: Building Smart Solutions with Python for Real-World Applications

Practical Use Cases: Web Scraping, APIs, and Automation

Web Scraping   APIs   Autonution

Python is one of the most versatile programming languages out there, known for its simplicity, readability, and power. Over the years, Python has become a go-to language for building **smart solutions** to a wide variety of real-world problems. Whether it's automating repetitive tasks, scraping useful data from websites, or interacting with external web services via **APIs** (Application Programming Interfaces), Python makes it easier to solve everyday challenges efficiently.

In this chapter, we'll explore practical Python use cases such as **web scraping, working with APIs**, and **automation**. These are powerful techniques that can be used to extract information, interact with remote servers, and automate time-consuming tasks. Python's extensive set of libraries and tools make these tasks accessible and easy to implement.

We'll also look at how Python can help analyze and solve real-world problems across various domains like data extraction, task automation, and more. By the end of this chapter, you will understand how to use Python to interact with external web services and automate tasks effectively.

Understanding Web Scraping and Its Real-World Applications

Web scraping is the process of automatically extracting data from websites. Websites are designed to display information in a way that is easy for humans to read but not necessarily easy for machines to parse. Web scraping helps convert this human-readable data into a structured format that can be analyzed, processed, and used for further tasks, such as building databases, generating reports, or performing research.

Common Web Scraping Applications:

- **Price comparison**: Scraping product prices from e-commerce websites to compare and find the best deals.
- **Market research**: Extracting product descriptions, reviews, and other data from online stores.
- **Job listings**: Scraping job portals for the latest job openings, salary data, and company reviews.
- **Social media data**: Collecting publicly available social media data for sentiment analysis or other research purposes.

Web Scraping with Python

Python is a fantastic language for web scraping, thanks to libraries like **BeautifulSoup, Requests**, and **Selenium**. These libraries allow you to extract data from websites easily, parse HTML content, and interact with dynamic content like JavaScript-rendered pages.

Here's an overview of the libraries we'll use:

- **Requests**: Used to send HTTP requests to fetch web pages.
- **BeautifulSoup**: A Python library for parsing HTML and XML documents. It provides methods for navigating and searching through the parsed page structure.
- **Selenium**: Used for scraping dynamic websites that require interaction with JavaScript, such as clicking buttons or filling out forms.

Step 1: Installing the Required Libraries

First, you need to install the necessary libraries. If you don't have them installed, you can install them via pip:

bash

```
pip install requests beautifulsoup4
```

If you plan on scraping dynamic pages that require interacting with JavaScript, you may also want to install **Selenium**:

bash

```
pip install selenium
```

Additionally, for Selenium to interact with browsers, you'll need to download a driver for your browser (e.g., ChromeDriver for Google Chrome).

Step 2: Sending HTTP Requests to Fetch Web Pages

The `requests` library is commonly used to retrieve web pages. It allows you to send HTTP requests and handle the response. Here's an example of how to fetch a webpage:

python

```python
import requests

# Send an HTTP GET request to the website
response = requests.get('https://example.com')

# Check if the request was successful
if response.status_code == 200:
    print("Successfully fetched the webpage!")
    print(response.text)  # The HTML content of the
webpage
else:
    print("Failed to fetch the webpage.")
```

Step 3: Parsing HTML with BeautifulSoup

Once you have fetched the page, you can parse the HTML content using **BeautifulSoup**. This allows you to navigate the HTML structure and extract the data you need.

python

```python
from bs4 import BeautifulSoup

# Parse the HTML content using BeautifulSoup
soup = BeautifulSoup(response.text, 'html.parser')

# Find all headings in the page
headings = soup.find_all('h2')
```

```
for heading in headings:
    print(heading.text)  # Print each heading text
```

In this example, we used BeautifulSoup to parse the HTML content and then extracted all the `<h2>` headings from the page.

Step 4: Extracting Data and Saving It

After extracting the relevant data, we can save it in a structured format like **CSV** for further analysis. Let's scrape some product information from an e-commerce website (hypothetical example) and save it into a CSV file:

```python
import csv

# Example: Scraping product names and prices from a
website
product_names = []
product_prices = []

# Assuming soup contains the parsed HTML content
products = soup.find_all('div', class_='product')  #
Assuming products are in divs with class 'product'

for product in products:
    name = product.find('h2').text
    price = product.find('span', class_='price').text
    product_names.append(name)
    product_prices.append(price)

# Writing to a CSV file
with open('products.csv', 'w', newline='') as file:
    writer = csv.writer(file)
    writer.writerow(['Product Name', 'Price'])  #
Write headers
    for name, price in zip(product_names,
product_prices):
```

```
writer.writerow([name, price])
```

In this case, we:

1. Extracted product names and prices from a webpage.
2. Stored the data in two lists.
3. Saved the data into a CSV file for further processing.

Step 5: Handling Dynamic Content with Selenium

Sometimes, web pages contain dynamic content that's loaded via JavaScript (e.g., product listings, comments, etc.). In such cases, **Selenium** comes to the rescue. Selenium automates browsers, allowing you to interact with elements on a page, such as clicking buttons and waiting for content to load.

Here's a simple example of using Selenium to load a page and extract data:

python

```python
from selenium import webdriver

# Initialize the WebDriver (e.g., Chrome)
driver =
webdriver.Chrome(executable_path='path_to_chromedrive
r')

# Navigate to the webpage
driver.get('https://example.com')

# Wait for the page to load
driver.implicitly_wait(10)  # Wait for up to 10
seconds for elements to load

# Extract the product names and prices
products =
driver.find_elements_by_class_name('product')
```

```
for product in products:
    name =
product.find_element_by_tag_name('h2').text
    price =
product.find_element_by_class_name('price').text
    print(f"Product: {name}, Price: {price}")

# Close the browser
driver.quit()
```

In this example, we used Selenium to launch a browser, navigate to a webpage, and wait for JavaScript content to load. We then extracted the product data and printed it to the console.

Introduction to APIs and How They Work

An **API** (Application Programming Interface) is a set of rules and protocols that allows software applications to communicate with each other. APIs are used extensively for interacting with remote web services, enabling your application to access features or data from another system.

There are two main types of APIs:

- **RESTful APIs**: Based on HTTP and are typically stateless and follow REST (Representational State Transfer) principles. These APIs return data in formats like **JSON** or **XML**.
- **SOAP APIs**: Based on XML and are more rigid in structure compared to RESTful APIs.

Using Python to Work with APIs

Python's `requests` library makes it incredibly easy to interact with APIs. You can send HTTP requests to an API, and the API will return data, typically in **JSON** format, which you can process and use in your Python application.

Here's an example of interacting with a public API (for demonstration purposes):

```python
import requests

# Send a GET request to a public API
response =
requests.get('https://api.openweathermap.org/data/2.5
/weather?q=London&appid=your_api_key')

# Check if the request was successful
if response.status_code == 200:
    data = response.json()  # Convert the JSON data
to a Python dictionary
    print(f"Weather in London:
{data['weather'][0]['description']}")
    print(f"Temperature: {data['main']['temp']}°C")
else:
    print("Failed to fetch data from the API.")
```

In this example, we fetched weather data for London using the OpenWeatherMap API. The data returned is in JSON format, which we parse using `.json()` and then extract the necessary information, such as the weather description and temperature.

Automating Tasks with Python

One of Python's strongest suits is its ability to automate repetitive tasks. Automation allows you to save time and reduce human error in tasks like data entry, web scraping, email notifications, and more.

Automating File Management

Python can automate file handling tasks like moving files, renaming them, and organizing them into directories.

For example, let's say you want to organize files in a folder by their extensions:

```python
import os
import shutil

# Directory where files are located
source_directory = '/path/to/source/directory'

# Directory where files should be moved based on
extension
destination_directory =
'/path/to/destination/directory'

# List all files in the source directory
files = os.listdir(source_directory)

for file in files:
    # Get the file extension
    file_extension = file.split('.')[-1]

    # Create a new folder for the file type if it
doesn't exist
    type_folder = os.path.join(destination_directory,
file_extension)
    if not os.path.exists(type_folder):
        os.makedirs(type_folder)

    # Move the file to the corresponding folder
    shutil.move(os.path.join(source_directory, file),
os.path.join(type_folder, file))
```

In this example, Python automatically organizes files into subdirectories based on their extensions, helping automate the task of file management.

Automating Email Sending

Let's automate sending email notifications using Python's **smtplib** module. Here's how you can send an email using a Gmail account:

```python
import smtplib
from email.mime.text import MIMEText
from email.mime.multipart import MIMEMultipart

# Email credentials
sender_email = 'your_email@gmail.com'
receiver_email = 'recipient_email@example.com'
password = 'your_email_password'

# Create the email content
message = MIMEMultipart()
message['From'] = sender_email
message['To'] = receiver_email
message['Subject'] = 'Automated Email'

# Email body
body = 'This is an automated email sent using
Python.'
message.attach(MIMEText(body, 'plain'))

# Send the email
try:
    with smtplib.SMTP('smtp.gmail.com', 587) as
server:
        server.starttls()
        server.login(sender_email, password)
        server.sendmail(sender_email, receiver_email,
message.as_string())
    print("Email sent successfully!")
```

```
except Exception as e:
    print(f"Failed to send email: {e}")
```

In this example, we used Python's `smtplib` to connect to Gmail's SMTP server and send an email to the recipient.

Hands-On Example: Scrape Data from a Website and Save It into a CSV File

Let's create a practical example to scrape data from a website and save it into a CSV file. In this case, we'll scrape data about books from an online bookstore.

Step 1: Install Necessary Libraries If you haven't installed the required libraries, use the following pip commands:

```bash
pip install requests beautifulsoup4
```

Step 2: Scrape Data and Save It into a CSV File

Here's a Python script to scrape book titles, authors, and prices from a sample bookstore and save the data into a CSV file:

```python
import requests
from bs4 import BeautifulSoup
import csv

# Send a GET request to the website
response = requests.get('http://books.toscrape.com/')

# Parse the HTML content using BeautifulSoup
soup = BeautifulSoup(response.text, 'html.parser')
```

```python
# Find all books on the page
books = soup.find_all('article',
class_='product_pod')

# Prepare the CSV file for writing
with open('books.csv', 'w', newline='') as file:
    writer = csv.writer(file)
    writer.writerow(['Title', 'Author', 'Price'])  #
Write header

    # Extract and write book data
    for book in books:
        title = book.find('h3').find('a')['title']
        author = book.find('p', class_='author').text
        price = book.find('p',
class_='price_color').text
        writer.writerow([title, author, price])

print("Data scraped and saved to books.csv
successfully.")
```

In this script:

- We used the `requests` library to fetch the webpage.
- We parsed the HTML content with **BeautifulSoup** to extract book titles, authors, and prices.
- We saved the scraped data into a CSV file using the `csv` module.

Conclusion

In this chapter, we've explored how Python can be used to solve real-world problems through web scraping, working with APIs, and automating repetitive tasks. Python's powerful libraries, such as **Requests, BeautifulSoup, Selenium**, and **Smtplib**, make it incredibly easy to interact with external web services, process data, and automate everyday tasks.

We walked through several practical examples, including:

- Scraping book data from a website and saving it to a CSV file.
- Using APIs to retrieve real-time weather data.
- Automating email sending and file management.

By mastering these techniques, you can build smarter, more efficient solutions for a wide range of applications, from data extraction and task automation to interacting with web services. Python's flexibility and ease of use make it an ideal choice for building these smart solutions.

Chapter 13: Advanced Problem Solving: Dynamic Programming and Graph Algorithms

Understanding Dynamic Programming and Graph Algorithms

When you're tackling complex problems in programming, especially those that involve optimization or large datasets, simple iterative solutions often don't cut it. This is where more sophisticated problem-solving techniques like **Dynamic Programming (DP)** and **Graph Algorithms** come into play. These advanced techniques are essential tools in any programmer's toolkit, allowing you to efficiently solve problems that would otherwise be computationally expensive or hard to manage.

In this chapter, we will explore **Dynamic Programming** (DP) and **Graph Algorithms**, two fundamental approaches that can help you solve complex problems with more efficient solutions. We will dive deep into these techniques, explain the core concepts behind them, and walk through practical problem-solving examples. By the end of this chapter, you will have a solid understanding of DP and graph algorithms, as well as hands-on experience implementing them to solve problems.

What is Dynamic Programming?

Dynamic Programming (DP) is a method used for solving problems by breaking them down into smaller sub-problems, solving each sub-problem once, and storing the solutions to avoid redundant computations. It is particularly useful in optimization problems where a recursive approach would lead to overlapping sub-problems, making the solution inefficient.

Core Concepts of Dynamic Programming

- **Overlapping Subproblems**: This refers to the property of a problem where the same sub-problems are solved multiple times during the process of finding the solution. Dynamic Programming solves each sub-problem once and stores the result (usually in a table) to avoid re-solving it.
- **Optimal Substructure**: A problem has an optimal substructure if the optimal solution to the problem can be constructed efficiently from the optimal solutions to its sub-problems. This means that a problem can be broken down into smaller sub-problems, and solving these sub-problems leads to an overall optimal solution.

Example Problem: The Knapsack Problem

The **0/1 Knapsack Problem** is a classic example of a problem that can be solved efficiently using Dynamic Programming.

You are given a set of items, each with a weight and a value, and you are tasked with determining the maximum value you can achieve by selecting a subset of these items, subject to a weight limit. You can either take an item or leave it, making it a 0/1 decision for each item.

Recursive Solution

A naive approach to solve this problem would be using recursion, where we try all combinations of items and choose the one with the highest value that fits within the weight limit. However, this approach has an exponential time complexity, as it solves the same sub-problems multiple times.

Dynamic Programming Solution

Dynamic Programming helps optimize this problem by storing the results of sub-problems and reusing them. Let's implement a solution for the 0/1 Knapsack Problem.

```python
def knapsack(weights, values, capacity):
    n = len(weights)
    dp = [[0 for _ in range(capacity + 1)] for _ in
range(n + 1)]

    for i in range(1, n + 1):
        for w in range(capacity + 1):
            if weights[i - 1] <= w:
                dp[i][w] = max(values[i - 1] + dp[i -
1][w - weights[i - 1]], dp[i - 1][w])
            else:
                dp[i][w] = dp[i - 1][w]

    return dp[n][capacity]

# Example usage
weights = [1, 3, 4, 5]
values = [1, 4, 5, 7]
capacity = 7
```

```
print(knapsack(weights, values, capacity))   # Output:
9
```

In this implementation, `dp[i][w]` represents the maximum value achievable with the first `i` items and a weight limit `w`. By filling in this table iteratively, we ensure that each sub-problem is solved only once, and the solution is computed efficiently.

What are Graph Algorithms?

A **graph** is a collection of nodes (also called vertices) and edges that connect pairs of nodes. Graphs are used to represent relationships or connections between objects. Graph algorithms are essential for solving problems related to networks, pathfinding, optimization, and much more.

Graph Terminology

- **Vertex**: A node in the graph.
- **Edge**: A connection between two vertices.
- **Directed vs. Undirected Graphs**: In a directed graph, edges have a direction, whereas in an undirected graph, edges have no direction.
- **Weighted Graph**: A graph where each edge has a weight or cost associated with it.

Graph Traversal Algorithms

Graph traversal is the process of visiting all the vertices of a graph in a particular order. There are two fundamental graph traversal algorithms:

1. **Depth-First Search (DFS)**: DFS explores as far as possible along each branch before backtracking. It can be implemented using recursion or a stack.

2. **Breadth-First Search (BFS)**: BFS explores all the neighbors of a vertex before moving on to the next level of neighbors. It can be implemented using a queue.

Let's take a closer look at how these algorithms work.

Depth-First Search (DFS)

Depth-First Search starts at a source vertex and explores as far as possible along each branch before backtracking. DFS can be implemented using a stack or recursion.

Here's the DFS algorithm implemented using recursion:

python

```python
# DFS implementation using recursion
def dfs(graph, start, visited=None):
    if visited is None:
        visited = set()

    visited.add(start)
    print(start, end=' ')

    for neighbor in graph[start]:
        if neighbor not in visited:
            dfs(graph, neighbor, visited)

# Example graph (adjacency list)
graph = {
    'A': ['B', 'C'],
    'B': ['A', 'D', 'E'],
    'C': ['A', 'F'],
    'D': ['B'],
    'E': ['B', 'F'],
    'F': ['C', 'E']
}

# Example usage: DFS starting from vertex 'A'
dfs(graph, 'A')
```

Output:

```
mathematica
```

```
A B D E F C
```

DFS explores all vertices starting from 'A', going as deep as possible along each branch before backtracking.

Breadth-First Search (BFS)

Breadth-First Search explores the graph level by level, starting from the source vertex. It uses a queue to keep track of vertices to explore.

Here's the BFS algorithm implemented using a queue:

```python
from collections import deque

# BFS implementation using a queue
def bfs(graph, start):
    visited = set()
    queue = deque([start])

    while queue:
        vertex = queue.popleft()
        if vertex not in visited:
            visited.add(vertex)
            print(vertex, end=' ')
            queue.extend(neighbor for neighbor in
graph[vertex] if neighbor not in visited)

# Example usage: BFS starting from vertex 'A'
bfs(graph, 'A')
```

Output:

```mathematica
A B C D E F
```

BFS explores all vertices at the present depth level before moving on to the next level, making it ideal for problems like finding the shortest path in an unweighted graph.

Solving Complex Problems with Dynamic Programming and Graph Algorithms

Now that we understand Dynamic Programming and Graph Algorithms, let's discuss how they can be applied to solve real-world problems.

Dynamic Programming Problem: Coin Change Problem

The **Coin Change Problem** asks for the minimum number of coins needed to make a certain amount of money, given a set of coin denominations. This is a classic problem that can be solved using dynamic programming.

Problem Statement: Given a list of coin denominations and a target amount, find the minimum number of coins needed to make the target amount.

Solution Using Dynamic Programming:

```python
def coin_change(coins, amount):
    # Create a table to store the minimum number of
coins for each amount
    dp = [float('inf')] * (amount + 1)
    dp[0] = 0  # No coins are needed to make 0

    for coin in coins:
        for i in range(coin, amount + 1):
```

```
        dp[i] = min(dp[i], dp[i - coin] + 1)

    return dp[amount] if dp[amount] != float('inf')
else -1

# Example usage
coins = [1, 2, 5]
amount = 11
print(coin_change(coins, amount))   # Output: 3 (11 =
5 + 5 + 1)
```

In this solution, we use a **bottom-up dynamic programming** approach to build up the solution. We create a table `dp` where `dp[i]` stores the minimum number of coins needed to make the amount `i`. For each coin, we update the table by checking whether including that coin results in a smaller number of coins for each amount.

Graph Problem: Shortest Path Using Dijkstra's Algorithm

Dijkstra's algorithm is used to find the shortest path from a source vertex to all other vertices in a **weighted graph**. It works by iteratively selecting the vertex with the smallest tentative distance and updating the distances to its neighbors.

Here's how we can implement Dijkstra's algorithm:

python

```
import heapq

def dijkstra(graph, start):
    # Create a priority queue (min-heap)
    queue = [(0, start)]   # (distance, vertex)
    distances = {vertex: float('inf') for vertex in
graph}
    distances[start] = 0
    visited = set()
```

```
    while queue:
        current_distance, current_vertex =
heapq.heappop(queue)

        if current_vertex in visited:
            continue

        visited.add(current_vertex)

        for neighbor, weight in
graph[current_vertex].items():
            distance = current_distance + weight
            if distance < distances[neighbor]:
                distances[neighbor] = distance
                heapq.heappush(queue, (distance,
neighbor))

    return distances

# Example graph (adjacency list with weights)
graph = {
    'A': {'B': 1, 'C': 4},
    'B': {'A': 1, 'C': 2, 'D': 5},
    'C': {'A': 4, 'B': 2, 'D': 1},
    'D': {'B': 5, 'C': 1}
}

# Example usage: Find shortest paths from 'A'
print(dijkstra(graph, 'A'))
```

Output:

arduino

```
{'A': 0, 'B': 1, 'C': 3, 'D': 4}
```

Dijkstra's algorithm efficiently computes the shortest path from the start vertex to all other vertices in the graph by exploring the neighbors and updating their tentative distances.

Hands-On Example: Solve a Dynamic Programming Problem (Coin Change) and Implement Graph Traversal

In this example, we'll combine both Dynamic Programming and Graph Algorithms to solve two separate problems.

Coin Change Problem (Dynamic Programming):

As shown earlier, we can solve the **Coin Change Problem** using dynamic programming. This approach works for problems where you need to find the **optimal solution** by breaking the problem down into sub-problems, solving them once, and storing their results.

Graph Traversal (DFS and BFS):

For the graph traversal part, we'll use both **DFS** and **BFS** to explore the graph. These algorithms are essential for understanding how data is traversed in a graph, which can be applied in various domains like search engines, network routing, and even social media analysis.

```python
def dfs(graph, start, visited=None):
    if visited is None:
        visited = set()
    visited.add(start)
    print(start, end=' ')
    for neighbor in graph[start]:
        if neighbor not in visited:
            dfs(graph, neighbor, visited)

def bfs(graph, start):
    visited = set()
    queue = [start]
```

```
        visited.add(start)

        while queue:
            vertex = queue.pop(0)
            print(vertex, end=' ')
            for neighbor in graph[vertex]:
                if neighbor not in visited:
                    visited.add(neighbor)
                    queue.append(neighbor)

# Example graph
graph = {
    'A': ['B', 'C'],
    'B': ['A', 'D', 'E'],
    'C': ['A', 'F'],
    'D': ['B'],
    'E': ['B', 'F'],
    'F': ['C', 'E']
}

# Perform DFS and BFS
print("DFS Traversal:")
dfs(graph, 'A')
print("\nBFS Traversal:")
bfs(graph, 'A')
```

Output:

```
mathematica

DFS Traversal:
A B D E F C
BFS Traversal:
A B C D E F
```

By applying **DFS** and **BFS**, you can traverse a graph and explore all its nodes, with DFS going deeper before backtracking and BFS exploring level by level.

Conclusion

In this chapter, we've covered two powerful problem-solving techniques: **Dynamic Programming (DP)** and **Graph Algorithms**. These methods are essential for efficiently solving complex problems in fields ranging from computer science and mathematics to engineering and finance.

We discussed how **Dynamic Programming** optimizes problems like the **Knapsack Problem** and the **Coin Change Problem** by breaking them into smaller sub-problems and storing the results for future use. We also examined graph algorithms like **DFS** and **BFS**, which are fundamental for exploring networks and finding the shortest path in graphs.

By implementing and understanding these algorithms, you now have the tools to solve complex problems efficiently. Whether you're working on optimization tasks, pathfinding in networks, or other computational problems, these techniques will serve as a solid foundation for your problem-solving skills.

Chapter 14: Cracking Coding Interviews with Python

Preparation Tips and Common Coding Interview Problems

Landing a job in tech often requires you to pass a **coding interview**, a critical step in the hiring process for many companies, especially in software engineering roles. These interviews typically focus on assessing your problem-solving skills, understanding of algorithms and data structures, and your ability to write clean, efficient code. A solid performance in a coding interview can demonstrate to employers that you are capable of tackling real-world problems with a methodical, analytical approach.

In this chapter, we will focus on **preparation tips** for coding interviews, highlight **common interview problems**, and provide **practical strategies** for approaching coding challenges. We'll also dive into a **hands-on example** that mirrors the kind of problem you might encounter during an interview. By the end of this chapter, you'll be better equipped to handle coding interviews with Python, thinking critically and solving problems efficiently.

What to Expect in a Coding Interview

In a typical coding interview, you can expect the following:

- **Problem-solving**: The interviewer will present a problem, and your task is to come up with a solution. The key is not just to solve the problem but to do so **efficiently** using the right data structures and algorithms.
- **Coding**: Once you have your solution, you'll be asked to write clean, working code to implement it. Pay attention to **edge cases** and **optimizations**.
- **Discussion**: After writing your code, the interviewer will typically ask you to explain your solution. Be prepared to talk through your reasoning, trade-offs, and alternatives.
- **Testing**: The interviewer might also ask you to test your code with different inputs, ensuring that it works correctly for all cases, including edge cases.

Key Areas Covered in Coding Interviews:

1. **Data Structures**: Arrays, linked lists, stacks, queues, hashmaps, trees, and graphs.
2. **Algorithms**: Sorting, searching, recursion, dynamic programming, and greedy algorithms.
3. **Time and Space Complexity**: Understanding Big O notation and optimizing your solution.

Best Practices for Approaching Coding Interview Questions

When you're presented with a coding problem in an interview, how you approach it is just as important as your ability to solve it. Here are some best practices for tackling coding interview problems:

1. Understand the Problem

- **Read carefully**: Make sure you fully understand the problem before jumping into a solution. Don't hesitate to ask the interviewer for clarification if something is unclear.
- **Restate the problem**: In your own words, explain the problem to the interviewer. This not only confirms that you've understood the problem but also sets the stage for your approach.
- **Identify inputs and outputs**: Clearly define the inputs and expected outputs. This will help you structure your solution.
- **Consider edge cases**: Think about potential edge cases or special scenarios that may break your solution (e.g., empty inputs, large inputs, negative values).

2. Break Down the Problem

- **Start simple**: If the problem seems complex, try to break it down into smaller, manageable parts. Solve the smaller pieces first.
- **Write pseudocode**: Before jumping into the actual coding, it's often helpful to write pseudocode or outline your approach. This helps you think through your solution without getting bogged down in syntax.
- **Choose the right data structure**: Selecting the appropriate data structure for the problem is key. For example, if you need fast lookups, a **hashmap** is a good choice; if you're dealing with a sequence of elements, consider an **array** or **list**.

3. Optimize Your Solution

- **Aim for efficiency**: In most coding interviews, the goal is not just to solve the problem but to solve it efficiently. Be mindful of the time and space complexity of your solution.
- **Big O analysis**: Understand how the time and space complexity of your solution scale with input size. Aim for solutions with **O(n)**, **O(log n)**, or **O(n log n)** time complexity, if possible.

4. Write Clean, Readable Code

- **Follow coding conventions**: Write code that is easy to read and maintain. Use clear variable names, add comments where necessary, and follow consistent indentation.
- **Avoid over-complicating things**: Don't try to use advanced features or overly complex solutions unless necessary. Keep your code simple and easy to understand.

5. Test Your Solution

- **Check for edge cases**: Make sure to test your solution with edge cases—empty inputs, large inputs, negative numbers, etc.
- **Walk through your code**: Mentally walk through your code with a set of test cases. This will help you identify bugs or inefficiencies before you run the code.
- **Explain your solution**: Be prepared to explain your code to the interviewer, including why you chose a particular approach, and how it works. If you encounter

issues during testing, discuss your thought process and potential solutions.

6. Practice, Practice, Practice

- **Solve problems regularly**: The best way to prepare for coding interviews is through consistent practice. Use websites like **LeetCode, HackerRank**, and **CodeSignal** to practice solving coding problems.
- **Simulate interview conditions**: Try solving problems within a time limit to simulate the pressure of an actual interview.

Common Coding Interview Problems

The following are common types of problems you might encounter in a coding interview. We'll go over how to approach them and provide a hands-on solution.

1. Array and String Manipulation

- Common problems: Find the maximum product of two numbers, reverse an array, check if a string is a palindrome.

2. Dynamic Programming

- Common problems: Coin change, longest common subsequence, 0/1 knapsack.

3. Graph Algorithms

- Common problems: Shortest path (Dijkstra's), depth-first search (DFS), breadth-first search (BFS), cycle detection.

4. Linked List Problems

- Common problems: Reverse a linked list, find the middle element, detect a cycle.

5. Sorting and Searching

- Common problems: Binary search, merge sort, quicksort, finding the kth largest element.

How to Think Like a Problem Solver During Interviews

During coding interviews, your ability to think critically and logically is what sets you apart. Here's how to develop that mindset:

1. Think Step-by-Step

Instead of diving into the code right away, take a moment to think about the problem. Break it down into smaller steps:

- What is the problem asking for?
- What are the constraints?
- What data structures could be useful?
- How will you handle edge cases?

By taking a structured approach, you'll avoid getting lost in unnecessary details and focus on the core problem.

2. Explore Multiple Solutions

There's usually more than one way to solve a problem. If you have time during the interview, it's often helpful to discuss multiple approaches:

- A brute force solution, followed by an optimized one.
- A recursive approach versus an iterative approach.
- A greedy solution versus a dynamic programming solution.

Each solution may have trade-offs in terms of time and space complexity. Being able to discuss and compare multiple solutions shows that you have a deep understanding of algorithms.

3. Be Open to Feedback

Don't be afraid to ask for help or clarify the problem if needed. If you get stuck, the interviewer may guide you in the right direction. They may also suggest alternative ways to approach the problem. Be open to suggestions and think critically about how they affect your solution.

4. Stay Calm Under Pressure

Interviews can be stressful, but maintaining a calm and focused attitude will help you think clearly. If you feel stuck, take a deep breath, step back, and reassess your approach. It's okay to make mistakes, as long as you can learn from them and correct them.

Hands-On Example: Solve an Interview-Style Problem

Let's work through a common coding interview problem: **"Find the first non-repeating character in a string."**

Problem Statement: Write a Python function that takes a string as input and returns the first non-repeating character. If no such character exists, return None.

For example:

- Input: "abacabad"
- Output: "c"

Step 1: Brute Force Approach

A brute force approach would be to check each character in the string and count its occurrences. If a character appears only once, return it. This approach has a time complexity of **O(n^2)**.

python

```python
def first_non_repeating_brute(s):
    for i in range(len(s)):
        if s.count(s[i]) == 1:
            return s[i]
    return None

# Example usage
print(first_non_repeating_brute("abacabad"))   #
Output: 'c'
```

Step 2: Optimized Approach Using a Hash Map

The brute force approach is inefficient, so let's optimize it. We can use a **hash map** (dictionary in Python) to count the frequency of each character in the string. Then, we can iterate through the string again and return the first character with a count of 1.

This approach has a time complexity of **O(n)**, which is much more efficient than the brute force approach.

```python
def first_non_repeating(s):
    char_count = {}

    # Count the frequency of each character
    for char in s:
        char_count[char] = char_count.get(char, 0) + 1

    # Find the first non-repeating character
    for char in s:
        if char_count[char] == 1:
            return char

    return None

# Example usage
print(first_non_repeating("abacabad"))  # Output: 'c'
```

Step 3: Explanation of the Code

- In the first loop, we count the frequency of each character and store it in the dictionary char_count.
- In the second loop, we check each character in the original string. The first character that appears only once is returned as the result.

- If no non-repeating character is found, the function returns `None`.

Step 4: Testing Edge Cases

It's important to test your solution with different edge cases:

- An empty string: `""`
- A string with all repeating characters: `"aabbcc"`
- A string with only one character: `"a"`

```python
print(first_non_repeating(""))          # Output:
None
print(first_non_repeating("aabbcc"))    # Output:
None
print(first_non_repeating("a"))         # Output: 'a'
```

This ensures that your solution handles a variety of inputs correctly.

Conclusion

In this chapter, we've covered essential **preparation tips** for coding interviews, explored **common coding problems**, and walked through strategies for approaching interview questions with confidence. We also demonstrated how to think like a problem solver, break down problems into smaller components, and choose the most efficient solutions.

Through our **hands-on example** of solving the "first non-repeating character in a string" problem, we learned how to approach problems systematically, optimize solutions for efficiency, and test our code for edge cases.

By practicing these techniques and mastering Python, you will be better prepared for your coding interviews and be able to solve complex problems with clarity and precision.

Chapter 15: Building Microservices and Scalable Python Applications

Designing and Implementing Microservices Architectures

In the world of modern software development, the need for **scalability** and **maintainability** has led to the adoption of **microservices architectures**. Microservices offer a way to break down a large, monolithic application into smaller, self-contained services that can be developed, deployed, and scaled independently. Each microservice focuses on a specific business capability and communicates with other services over lightweight protocols, such as HTTP or messaging queues.

In this chapter, we'll explore how to design and implement **microservices architectures** using **Python**. We will also introduce key tools like **Flask, Django**, and **Docker**, which are commonly used to build, deploy, and scale microservices in real-world applications.

By the end of this chapter, you'll understand the core concepts of **microservices**, how to build scalable Python applications, and how to deploy them using **Docker**. We'll work through a hands-on example of building a simple **REST API** using **Flask** and deploying it with Docker.

What Are Microservices?

Microservices is an architectural style that structures an application as a collection of small, independently deployable services. Each service in a microservices architecture is designed to perform a specific function and is typically designed around a business capability, such as **user authentication, payment processing**, or **inventory management**. Microservices communicate with each other over a network using protocols like **HTTP** and **REST**.

Key Characteristics of Microservices:

- **Independently Deployable**: Microservices are deployed independently, which means changes to one service don't affect others.
- **Domain-Driven**: Each service is focused on a specific business domain or capability, making it easier to maintain and scale.
- **Technology Agnostic**: Different microservices can use different programming languages, databases, or frameworks based on their requirements.
- **Fault Isolation**: Since each microservice operates independently, failure in one service doesn't bring down the entire system.
- **Scalability**: Microservices can be scaled independently, so you can allocate resources where needed based on demand.

Advantages of Microservices:

- **Improved maintainability**: Smaller codebases that are easier to understand and maintain.

- **Faster development cycles**: Independent services can be developed, tested, and deployed faster.
- **Resilience**: Failures in one service do not bring down the entire application.
- **Technology flexibility**: You can use different technologies for different services, which helps optimize performance and efficiency.

Challenges of Microservices:

- **Increased complexity**: Managing multiple services introduces complexity, especially when dealing with inter-service communication, data consistency, and security.
- **Distributed systems**: Microservices require managing multiple distributed systems, which can make debugging and monitoring more challenging.
- **Deployment overhead**: Microservices require sophisticated deployment strategies and infrastructure to manage their independence and scalability.

How to Build Scalable Applications Using Python and Microservices

Building scalable applications involves several steps. In the context of microservices, scalability refers to the ability of the application to handle increased traffic, workload, or data storage demands. Here are the steps involved in building scalable Python applications using microservices:

1. Identify Business Capabilities

The first step in building a microservices-based application is to identify and break down the application into smaller business domains. These domains typically align with specific features or services of the application. For example, in an e-commerce application, you might identify services like:

- **User management** (e.g., registration, login, user profile)
- **Product catalog** (e.g., managing products, categories, prices)
- **Order management** (e.g., processing orders, payment, shipment)

2. Design RESTful APIs for Communication

Each microservice communicates with other services through APIs, typically using **REST** (Representational State Transfer). REST APIs are lightweight and easy to integrate, making them ideal for microservices architectures. Here are key considerations for designing RESTful APIs:

- **Stateless**: Each request to the API should contain all the information needed to understand the request, without relying on any previous interactions.
- **Uniform Interface**: Define clear endpoints for each service, such as `POST /orders` for creating an order or `GET /products` for retrieving products.
- **Versioning**: Manage API versions to ensure backward compatibility when making changes to the services.

3. Decouple Services and Data Storage

Each microservice should manage its own data storage. This ensures that services are loosely coupled and can evolve independently. For example, the **user service** might use a relational database (e.g., MySQL), while the **product catalog service** might use a NoSQL database (e.g., MongoDB).

Decoupling services and data storage makes it easier to scale each service independently.

4. Use Docker for Containerization

Docker is a tool that allows you to package and deploy microservices as **containers**. A container is a lightweight, portable package that includes everything needed to run a service, such as the application code, libraries, and dependencies. Using Docker allows you to:

- Ensure consistency between different environments (development, testing, production).
- Isolate services for easier management and scaling.
- Simplify deployment and continuous integration/continuous deployment (CI/CD) pipelines.

5. Implement Service Discovery

In a microservices architecture, services need to find each other in a dynamic environment. **Service discovery** is a mechanism that helps services locate and communicate with each other. Common solutions for service discovery in microservices include:

- **Consul**: A tool for service discovery and configuration.
- **Eureka**: A service registry for service discovery in cloud-based microservices architectures.

6. Handle Communication Between Services

Microservices often need to communicate with each other. This can be done synchronously (using HTTP requests) or asynchronously (using message queues). Here are common approaches to service communication:

- **RESTful APIs (synchronous)**: Services communicate via HTTP requests, typically using JSON as the data format.
- **Message Queues (asynchronous)**: Tools like **RabbitMQ** or **Kafka** allow services to communicate asynchronously by sending messages to queues. This approach is suitable for decoupling services and improving scalability.

Introduction to Tools Like Flask, Django, and Docker for Deployment

Flask: Lightweight Framework for Microservices

Flask is a lightweight Python web framework that is widely used for building microservices. It provides the flexibility to build small, simple applications that can scale as needed. Flask is particularly well-suited for building RESTful APIs because it offers minimal overhead and gives developers full control over how they structure their applications.

Flask provides the following advantages for building microservices:

- **Simplicity**: Flask is minimalistic, allowing developers to add only the components they need.
- **Extensibility**: Flask has a rich ecosystem of extensions that can add features such as authentication, database integration, and form validation.

- **Flexibility**: Flask allows you to define your own application structure and doesn't impose any particular design patterns, which is ideal for microservices.

Django: Full-Stack Framework for Building Scalable Applications

Django is a full-stack Python web framework that follows the Model-View-Template (MVT) architectural pattern. Django provides a more opinionated structure than Flask and comes with built-in features for building scalable web applications. It is a good choice when you need to build a full-featured web application with authentication, database management, and other common web application components.

While Django is generally used for monolithic applications, it can also be used in a microservices architecture, where each service is a separate Django application. The Django REST framework can be used to build robust RESTful APIs for communication between microservices.

Docker: Containerization for Microservices

Docker is an essential tool for building, deploying, and managing microservices. Docker allows you to create **containers** that package an application and its dependencies into a single, portable unit. Containers can run on any platform that supports Docker, ensuring consistency across development, testing, and production environments.

The key benefits of Docker for microservices are:

- **Isolation**: Each microservice runs in its own container, ensuring that it is isolated from others.

- **Portability**: Docker containers can run anywhere, whether it's on a developer's local machine, a test environment, or in production.
- **Scalability**: Containers are lightweight, so they can be quickly spun up or down to meet changing demand.

Hands-On Example: Build a Simple REST API Using Flask and Deploy It with Docker

In this section, we will walk through the process of building a simple **REST API** using **Flask** and deploying it with **Docker**.

Step 1: Install Flask

To begin, you need to install Flask. You can do this by running:

```bash
pip install flask
```

Step 2: Create a Simple Flask Application

Next, create a file called `app.py` and add the following code to define a basic REST API:

```python
from flask import Flask, jsonify

app = Flask(__name__)

# A simple route to return a welcome message
@app.route('/')
def welcome():
    return "Welcome to the Microservices API!"
```

```
# A route to get a list of products (simulating a
product catalog)
@app.route('/products', methods=['GET'])
def get_products():
    products = [
        {'id': 1, 'name': 'Laptop', 'price': 999.99},
        {'id': 2, 'name': 'Smartphone', 'price':
699.99},
        {'id': 3, 'name': 'Tablet', 'price': 399.99}
    ]
    return jsonify(products)

if __name__ == '__main__':
    app.run(debug=True)
```

This simple Flask application defines two routes:

1. / – A basic welcome message.
2. /products – A list of sample products returned as a JSON response.

Step 3: Test the Flask Application

Run the Flask application locally:

```
bash
```

```
python app.py
```

You should see output indicating the application is running:

```
csharp
```

```
 * Running on http://127.0.0.1:5000/ (Press CTRL+C to
quit)
```

Visit http://127.0.0.1:5000/ in your web browser, and you should see the welcome message. Visit `http://127.0.0.1:5000/products` to view the product list in JSON format.

Step 4: Create a Dockerfile for the Flask Application

Now, let's containerize this Flask application using Docker. Create a file named `Dockerfile` in the same directory as your `app.py` with the following content:

```dockerfile
# Use an official Python runtime as a parent image
FROM python:3.8-slim

# Set the working directory in the container
WORKDIR /app

#  the current directory contents into the container
at /app
 . /app

# Install any needed packages specified in
requirements.txt
RUN pip install --no-cache-dir -r requirements.txt

# Make port 5000 available to the world outside the
container
EXPOSE 5000

# Define environment variable
ENV FLASK_APP=app.py

# Run Flask when the container launches
CMD ["flask", "run", "--host", "0.0.0.0"]
```

This `Dockerfile`:

1. Uses the official Python 3.8 image as the base image.
2. Copies the application files into the container.
3. Installs the dependencies from `requirements.txt`.

4. Exposes port 5000 (the default port for Flask).
5. Runs the Flask application when the container starts.

Step 5: Create a requirements.txt File

Create a `requirements.txt` file to specify the required Python packages. Add the following content:

```
nginx

flask
```

Step 6: Build the Docker Image

Now, you can build the Docker image by running the following command in the terminal:

```bash
docker build -t flask-microservice .
```

This command builds the Docker image and tags it as `flask-microservice`.

Step 7: Run the Docker Container

After building the image, run the container with the following command:

```bash
docker run -p 5000:5000 flask-microservice
```

Your Flask application is now running inside a Docker container. You can visit `http://127.0.0.1:5000/products` to check the list of products served by the containerized application.

Conclusion

In this chapter, we explored **microservices architectures** and how to implement them using Python. We also looked at how to build scalable applications using Python, **Flask**, and **Docker**.

We started with the core concepts of microservices and discussed how to design and implement microservices in Python. We also learned how to build RESTful APIs using Flask and deploy them using Docker, making our microservices scalable and easy to manage. This hands-on approach to building and deploying a simple Flask-based REST API demonstrates how to get started with Python microservices development.

By applying the knowledge gained in this chapter, you will be able to design, implement, and deploy scalable Python-based microservices and develop systems that can handle growth and complexity with ease. With **Docker** enabling easy deployment and management, and **Flask** providing a lightweight framework for building microservices, Python is an excellent choice for building robust, scalable applications in today's cloud-native world.

Conclusion: Empowering You to Solve Problems Like a Pro

Reviewing Key Concepts

As we reach the end of this journey through the world of Python programming, it's essential to take a step back and reflect on everything you've learned so far. From your initial exposure to Python syntax and basic concepts to the advanced techniques like **dynamic programming, graph algorithms**, and **microservices,** you've covered a broad range of topics that are integral to becoming an expert problem solver. This conclusion will serve as a reminder of the core concepts you've mastered and offer you practical advice on how to continue building your skills.

The Fundamentals: Python Syntax and Problem Solving

At the core of Python programming lies a deep understanding of its syntax and how to write clean, efficient code. Throughout this book, we've seen how Python's simplicity allows you to quickly get started with writing code, making it an excellent language for both beginners and experienced developers. The key to solving any programming problem is breaking it down into smaller, more manageable parts and applying the right solution efficiently. You've learned how to:

- Use **variables, loops,** and **conditionals** to control the flow of your program.

- Understand **data structures** such as **lists, dictionaries, sets**, and **tuples**, and how to manipulate them to suit your needs.
- Apply basic **algorithmic techniques** such as sorting and searching to solve everyday problems.
- Write **functions** to create reusable, modular code that can be used across your applications.

These foundational concepts are the bedrock of all problem-solving in Python. With a firm understanding of them, you can approach almost any programming challenge with confidence.

Dynamic Programming and Optimization

As you've learned, some problems are inherently more complex and require advanced techniques to solve efficiently. **Dynamic programming (DP)** is one such technique. DP is used to solve optimization problems by breaking them down into smaller sub-problems and storing the results of those sub-problems to avoid redundant calculations. We've explored examples like the **coin change problem**, the **knapsack problem**, and how to approach these challenges using DP techniques such as **memoization** and **tabulation**.

Dynamic programming is a powerful tool that allows you to find **optimal solutions** to problems with overlapping subproblems, which is essential for handling larger datasets and more complex algorithms. Understanding how and when to apply DP to your problems will significantly improve your ability to solve a wide variety of challenges, especially when you need to handle large inputs or make decisions in real-time systems.

Graph Algorithms: Navigating Networks and Connections

Graph algorithms are another key area of expertise that you've gained throughout this journey. **Graphs** are an essential data structure used to model relationships and networks in fields ranging from computer networks to social media analysis and beyond. In this book, we've covered fundamental graph algorithms like **breadth-first search (BFS)** and **depth-first search (DFS)**, which allow you to traverse a graph and explore its structure.

Additionally, we've delved into **shortest path algorithms** like **Dijkstra's algorithm**, which is used to find the quickest route between two points in a graph. These algorithms are crucial when solving problems involving navigation, routing, and optimizing network performance.

Building Scalable Solutions with Microservices and Python

Building scalable applications is one of the most in-demand skills in the modern software development landscape. **Microservices architectures** allow you to break down large, monolithic applications into smaller, independently deployable services. Throughout this book, you've learned how to design and implement **Python microservices** using frameworks like **Flask** and **Django**, as well as how to deploy those services with **Docker**.

Microservices architectures are perfect for building applications that need to handle high traffic loads, evolve over time, and scale independently. By understanding how to design and implement microservices, you'll be equipped to build modern, scalable, and resilient applications that can grow and evolve with the needs of your users and customers.

Web Scraping and API Integration: Extracting Data and
Interfacing with External Systems

In today's data-driven world, **data extraction** and **integration**
with external services are fundamental skills. Through **web
scraping**, you've learned how to extract valuable data from
websites and APIs, enabling you to automate data collection,
research, and reporting tasks. With **Python libraries** like
BeautifulSoup, **Requests**, and **Selenium**, you can scrape
information from static and dynamic web pages and process
that data for use in your applications.

You've also learned how to interact with **RESTful APIs**,
enabling your applications to communicate with external
services, retrieve data, and perform actions based on that
data. From **weather APIs** to **social media integrations**,
understanding how to consume external data and interact with
APIs opens up a wealth of possibilities for building powerful
applications.

The Journey from Beginner to Expert Problem Solver

You've come a long way since the beginning of your journey,
and now you're equipped with the tools and knowledge to
tackle more advanced and complex programming problems.
However, becoming an expert problem solver doesn't happen
overnight. It requires consistent practice, critical thinking, and
the willingness to embrace new challenges.

From Basic Syntax to Complex Algorithms

The path from beginner to expert problem solver involves a natural progression of learning. Initially, you focus on mastering the **basics of Python syntax**, like variables, loops, and conditionals, which form the foundation of all programming tasks. From there, you move on to more advanced concepts, such as working with **data structures** and **algorithms**, and learning how to optimize your solutions for performance.

As you gain experience, you start solving **real-world problems** and building **scalable applications** using tools like **Flask**, **Django**, and **Docker**. This process not only helps you improve your technical skills but also develops your **problem-solving mindset**. Every time you solve a problem, you get better at breaking it down, selecting the right tools, and coming up with efficient solutions.

Critical Thinking: The Key to Problem Solving

Problem solving is not just about coding—it's about **thinking critically**. Every problem has multiple possible solutions, and the key to solving it efficiently lies in evaluating these solutions and choosing the one that is both effective and optimal. Here are some aspects of critical thinking that can help you excel as a problem solver:

1. **Breaking Down Problems**: The first step in solving any problem is breaking it down into smaller, more manageable parts. Instead of tackling a complex problem all at once, try to simplify it by isolating individual components.

2. **Analyzing Constraints**: Every problem comes with constraints. For example, a time limit, memory limit, or specific input types. Understanding these constraints is crucial for developing an efficient solution.
3. **Exploring Multiple Solutions**: Many problems have more than one solution. It's important to explore different approaches and analyze the trade-offs, such as time and space complexity, readability, and maintainability.
4. **Testing and Refining**: Once you have a solution, it's important to test it thoroughly with different inputs, including edge cases, to ensure it works as expected. Debugging is a crucial part of the problem-solving process.
5. **Learning from Mistakes**: Every mistake you make is an opportunity to learn and improve. Embrace failure as a stepping stone toward mastery, and always look for ways to optimize and refine your solutions.

Practical Advice for Continuing Your Python Learning Journey

The journey from beginner to expert in Python is ongoing, and there are always new skills to learn and explore. Here are some practical tips to help you continue your Python learning journey and deepen your understanding of the language and its applications.

1. Practice Regularly

The most effective way to become proficient in Python and problem-solving is through consistent practice. Websites like **LeetCode, HackerRank,** and **Codewars** offer a vast array of coding problems that will challenge you and help you improve your skills. By solving problems regularly, you'll reinforce your understanding of algorithms and data structures, and learn new techniques along the way.

2. Build Real-World Projects

Building real-world projects is an excellent way to put your knowledge into practice. Whether it's a web application, a data analysis tool, or a microservice-based system, working on projects helps you apply what you've learned in a practical, hands-on way. It also teaches you how to design scalable, maintainable systems and solve problems that arise in production environments.

3. Contribute to Open Source

Contributing to open-source projects is a great way to deepen your Python knowledge, collaborate with other developers, and give back to the community. Open-source projects often involve complex problems, and by contributing, you'll gain experience solving real-world challenges while working in a collaborative environment.

4. Learn New Python Libraries and Frameworks

Python has a rich ecosystem of libraries and frameworks that make it easy to solve a wide variety of problems. From **NumPy** for numerical computing to **TensorFlow** for machine learning, there's always something new to explore. As you continue learning, consider exploring these libraries to broaden your skillset and tackle more advanced topics.

5. Stay Curious and Keep Learning

The world of Python and programming is constantly evolving. New libraries, tools, and techniques are developed every day. To stay ahead, keep exploring new topics, experimenting with new libraries, and learning from others in the community. Attend meetups, read books, and follow blogs to stay up-to-date with the latest trends.

Next Steps for Real-World Applications

Now that you have a strong foundation in Python, problem-solving, and software development, it's time to apply your skills to real-world scenarios. Here are some next steps to help you transition from learning to applying Python in various domains:

1. Web Development

Python is widely used in web development, particularly with frameworks like **Flask** and **Django**. Whether you're building a RESTful API or a full-featured web application, Python makes web development fast, scalable, and efficient. Explore the possibilities of building production-ready applications and deploying them with modern technologies like **Docker, Kubernetes**, and **cloud services**.

2. Data Science and Machine Learning

Python is the go-to language for data science and machine learning, thanks to powerful libraries like **Pandas, NumPy, Scikit-learn**, and **TensorFlow**. If you're interested in data analysis, predictive modeling, or artificial intelligence, Python offers a wide range of tools to analyze and manipulate data, train machine learning models, and build intelligent systems.

3. Automation

Automation is one of Python's strongest suits. With libraries like **Selenium, BeautifulSoup,** and **APScheduler,** you can automate tedious tasks such as web scraping, file management, and even system monitoring. Python's ability to interface with APIs, databases, and file systems makes it an excellent choice for automation in almost any field.

4. Cloud and Microservices

As cloud computing and microservices become more prevalent, Python is increasingly being used to build scalable, cloud-native applications. By learning **cloud platforms** like **AWS**, **Google Cloud**, or **Azure**, and technologies like **Docker** and **Kubernetes**, you can deploy, manage, and scale your Python applications in a cloud environment.

5. Contribute to Python Communities

As a Python developer, one of the most valuable things you can do is engage with the wider Python community. Contribute to open-source projects, attend conferences, participate in forums like **Stack Overflow,** and help others solve their programming problems. This not only helps you grow as a developer but also allows you to give back to the community that's helped you along the way.

Conclusion

In this book, we've covered a wide range of topics that will help you evolve from a beginner to a skilled problem solver. You've learned essential Python concepts, from basic syntax and data structures to advanced topics like **dynamic programming, graph algorithms**, and **microservices architectures**. You've gained practical experience solving problems and building scalable, real-world applications.

But your journey doesn't end here. The key to mastering Python and becoming an expert problem solver is continuous learning, hands-on practice, and the willingness to embrace new challenges. Keep solving problems, building projects, and pushing yourself to explore new domains, and you'll be well on your way to becoming a Python expert.

The Python community is vast, and there are endless opportunities for growth. Whether you're working on web development, machine learning, automation, or cloud computing, Python offers the tools and libraries you need to succeed. Keep learning, keep building, and most importantly, keep solving problems like a pro.